Advance Praise for *It's Complicated*

"In this easy-to-read book, Pastor Jack Haberer helps you seek God's will for your life. You'll move from deep theological considerations to street-level, daily-life practicalities—and you'll learn to chart a course through life's complexities, guided by the Scriptures and in the company of the church. My only complaint is that it wasn't available thirty years ago!"
—Brian D. McLaren, Author/Speaker/Activist (brianmclaren.net)

"In his long and distinguished ministry and leadership in the church, Jack Haberer has demonstrated, time and time again, his commitment not only to traditional Christian morality but also to brothers and sisters who come to different and diverse conclusions. As he always does, in *It's Complicated* Haberer brings his evangelical faith into generous dialogue with the incredibly complex world in which we all live. This thoughtful book is based on the fundamental biblical tension between the goodness of creation and humankind's persistent failure to live up to the Creator's expectations, and it invites us to engage Scripture deeply, with openness to nuance. As such, the book will be a valuable resource and inspiration to all theological camps and ecclesiastical tribes to live responsibly, morally, and faithfully in our complicated world."
—John Buchanan, Former Publisher, *The Christian Century*

"Jack Haberer's new book *It's Complicated* is a thoughtful, provocative, and highly accessible resource for Christians with practical questions about how to live faithfully and ethically. Such living, after all, is complicated, as this book acknowledges. When all is said and done, the Bible is not just in conversation with us but also—always—in deep and serious conversation with itself. Haberer invites us into that conversation in ways that are understandable, encouraging, and finally joyful. This book breaks new ground. It is well worth reading!"
—Theodore J. Wardlaw, President, Austin Presbyterian Theological Seminary

"Jack has written a 'space-creating' book. In other words, even if you were to disagree with a way he interprets either a passage of Scripture or a current cultural issue, Jack has made space for you to stand without feeling backed into a corner. In a polarized and fearful world, that space is a gift. By helping the reader dig deeply into the complex Reformed understanding of the authority of Scripture, Jack helps us to remember that even the Bible itself creates space for different interpretations of how the living Word intersects our lives. This book will be of great use for the church and could help us change the ways in which we speak to one another."
—Shannon Kershner, Pastor, Fourth Presbyterian Church, Chicago

"Jack Haberer tackles the oft-ignored subject of how Christ followers rarely practice exactly what they readily acknowledge the Bible preaches. Yet he digs deep into Old and New Testaments to demonstrate that our best-effort instincts of how to behave as Christians are often, in fact, solidly biblical, even if the end result fails to score full points for precise obedience to particular divine directives. Haberer does not merely excuse us for the white lie of telling our mother-in-law that her green-bean casserole is delicious when it tastes like plaster. He helps us understand that people of faith from the book of Genesis to the present, including Jesus, regularly adapt our behavior to the meaning and contexts we face in order to be as faithful as possible to the Bible's demands that we love God and neighbor above all else. Haberer does all of this without reducing our biblical ethics to a cultural or situational relativism. Instead, he calls people of faith to a truly thoughtful, holistic, and brutally honest assessment of what God requires of us and how we might best achieve that in the messy, complicated, and often-convoluted events that collectively make up life. This clever and fresh approach to navigating life's ethical and moral decisions offers us reassuring biblical boundaries, interpreted via the Bible itself, good sense, and consoling human experience. Ultimately, Haberer offers a morally earnest Judeo-Christian ethic, grounded in Scripture, forged in reality, and saturated in God's hope and grace. Read it. It will do your heart and your life good!"
—Tom Taylor, President and CEO, Presbyterian Foundation

"'Compassionate' is the watchword of this timely book by Jack Haberer. As a pastor, he is known for his ability to bring 'liberals' and 'conservatives' together, encouraging them to focus on commonalities in order to deepen in relationship to one another. As editor of the *Presbyterian Outlook* during a turbulent time in the life of the Presbyterian Church (U.S.A.), he helped disputing parties listen to one another and represent one another in the fairest possible way. In this book he offers us the chance to participate in his thought processes as he struggles with complex issues such as abortion, euthanasia, capital punishment, interfaith marriage, and gay marriage. 'Life happens,' he says. Grace abounds, he reminds us. To be faithful to the gospel, he attests, is to hold fast to the truths we affirm, but never at the expense of the people we love and serve."
—Cynthia L. Rigby, W. C. Brown Professor of Theology, Austin Presbyterian Theological Seminary

"*It's Complicated: A Guide to Faithful Decision Making* is the proverbial grain of sand in the oyster. Jack Haberer's line of reasoning may irritate you to no end until you realize that a precious pearl has begun to form. Give it time—allow his ideas to ignite your imagination—and you'll realize that what he's proposing here might just be the way Jesus intended us to engage tough situations and difficult decisions all along."
—Jodi Craiglow, PhD candidate, Trinity Evangelical Divinity School Adjunct Professor, Trinity International University

"There is a precious and rare intersection at the crossing points of biblical ethics, practical application, and historical interpretation. Jack Haberer has defined this intersection and given his readers both the biblical tools and the practical structure to cultivate this precious ground in their own work and lives. I can easily imagine this book becoming a valued tool in many churches and Bible studies. In resisting the all-too-easy and all-too-binary answers that so many in our media and academies are willing to provide, Jack has produced a framework for conversation and discovery for the real world. The world that is varying shades of gray, the world where the rest of us must live."
—Christopher Edmonston, Pastor, White Memorial Presbyterian Church, Raleigh, North Carolina

"I celebrate Jack Haberer's contribution to this ongoing dialogue on interpreting and applying Scripture to contemporary issues that are dividing us. He combines the best of our pastoral, prophetic, and scholarly insights. He leads with authority without being authoritarian. This is a must-read for all those who are struggling to discern the will of Christ within church communities and amid a pluralistic culture with fidelity and integrity to the Word of God."

—Gary Demarest, Pastor, Author, Retired Associate Director of Evangelism, PC(USA)

It's Complicated

It's Complicated

A Guide to Faithful Decision Making

Jack Haberer

WESTMINSTER
JOHN KNOX PRESS
LOUISVILLE · KENTUCKY

First edition
Published by Westminster John Knox Press
Louisville, Kentucky

16 17 18 19 20 21 22 23 24 25—10 9 8 7 6 5 4 3 2 1

Book design by Sharon Adams
Cover design by Marc Whitaker / MTWdesign.net

Library of Congress Cataloging-in-Publication Data
Names: Haberer, Jack.
Title: It's complicated : a guide to faithful decision making / Jack Haberer.
Description: Louisville, KY : Westminster John Knox Press, 2016.
Identifiers: LCCN 2015036794 | ISBN 9780664261245 (alk. paper)
Subjects: LCSH: Decision making—Religious aspects—Christianity.
Classification: LCC BV4509.5 .H24 2016 | DDC 248.4—dc23 LC record available at http://lccn.loc.gov/2015036794

Most Westminster John Knox Press books are available at special quantity discounts when purchased in bulk by corporations, organizations, and special-interest groups. For more information, please e-mail SpecialSales@wjkbooks.com.

*She was educated by the Jesuits from kindergarten through college.
After earning a master's degree at Columbia University,
she became the first professor of psychology at a community college.
She taught her four children how to think.*

*Two years into that teaching role, she added to her schedule the
launching of a preschool for a minority community that would
morph into one of the first Head Start programs (she was ahead
of her time). She taught her children to care for the less fortunate.*

*Years later, while still teaching at the college, she converged her
psychological expertise with an ever-deepening faith to become one
of the pioneers of inner-healing prayer and shared that gift with
anyone seeking to be freed from their worst wounds. She taught her
adult children how to facilitate the healing of broken lives.*

*I am one of those four children. This book could not have been
written apart from all that she taught me. For these reasons
and many more, I dedicate this book to my mom,
Maureen Hastings Haberer (1924–2015), whom I miss terribly.*

Contents

Acknowledgments

As I will explain in chapter 7, this book has been brewing for nearly thirty years. Accordingly, many, many folks have helped give it life. In the beginning it was Carol Rootsey and Becky Cavallucci, both elders in my first congregation, who pushed me to share the first kernel ideas with the church's elders. On their prompting, the other elders gave a surprisingly enthusiastic endorsement vote (I then swore them to silence!). Other encouragements arose from other friends in Trinity Presbyterian Church, Satellite Beach, Florida, such as Hartley and Brenda Caldwell, Doug and Ruth Paauwe, Scott and Trisha Jordan.

In Clear Lake Presbyterian Church, Houston, Texas, these thoughts grew, fostered by conversations with associate pastors Barbara Carmichael, Jim Elder, Craig Goodwin, Nancy Goodwin; educators Connie Nyquist and Katrina Pennington (now a pastor); and our home-group friends, Jimmy and Marilu McGregor, Lynn and Julie Calhoun, George and Joyce Coyer, Will and Allison Groten, Jimmy and Suzette Connell, Mike and Susie Ray, plus prayer partners, Byder Wilde, Judy Franklin, Mary-Anne Collins, and Perry Westerfield.

In years of denominational service, I dialogued on so many pieces of this puzzle with Betty Moore; pastors Clayton Bell, John Huffman, David Snellgrove, Mort McMillan, Joseph Small (he helped me land on the terms *approximations* and *adaptations*), Sheldon Sorge; and my covenant brothers, pastors Jack Baca, Bob Henley, David Stoker, Hal Oakley, John Gable, Rich McDermott, and George Cladis.

As a member of the Presbyterian Church's Theological Task Force on Peace, Unity, and Purity of the Church, with whom I was in conversation for five years, the thesis of the book took flight, thanks to the intense and widely scrutinized (via the press) discussions with Mike Loudon, Gary Demarest, Victoria Curtiss, Stacy Johnson, Frances Taylor Gench, Barbara Wheeler (who impressed upon me the aspirational aspect of the commandments), John Wilkinson, Sarah Sanderson-Doughty, Joseph Coalter, Elizabeth Achtemeier, Mark Achtemeier, Jong Hyeong Lee, Scott Anderson, Barbara Everitt Bryant, Joan Merritt, Lonnie Oliver, Martha Sadongei, Jenny Stoner, Jose Luis Torres-Milan, and Mary Ellen Lawson.

As editor of *Presbyterian Outlook*, I enjoyed conversations with dialogue partners who fueled my brain. Chief among them was (and remains) Robert Johnson, PhD in theology and president of Friends of Forman Christian College, Lahore, Pakistan. In addition to our one-on-one conversations, our study group in the Foundation for Reformed Theology—pastors Mark Mueller, Agnes Brady, Ed Hurley, and Shawn Smith—hashed through some great discussions on these topics.

Also intense with conversation has been Tom Taylor, pastor, lawyer, scholar, and president of the Presbyterian Foundation. My colleagues on the *Presbyterian Outlook* staff added so much: Leslie Scanlon, George Whipple, Jana Blazek, Martha Skelton, Patricia Gresham, and Stann Bailey. Board members such as Quinn Fox, Laura Mendenhall, Richard Ray, John Wimberly, Mindy Douglas Adams, Judy Cutting, Christopher Edmonston, Matthew Rich, Joan Gray, Alex Evans, Fred Denson, Jill Duffield, Sallie Roberts, Syngman Rhee, Tom Currie, Jenny McDevitt, and Fairfax Fair all kept my brain in high gear. The number of readers who affirmed and challenged me number in the hundreds. Thanks go to them all.

Upon my return to Houston, my successor, pastor Steve Oglesbee, welcomed me back to Clear Lake Church and even invited me to lecture through the book—ten lectures plus four dialogue sessions. Terry Stone, an engineer by trade, co-taught the class and was simply outstanding. My Houston pastors' covenant group there brought great dialogue—I made one of my first presentations on this integrative Christian ethic to them, and they came back with lots of ideas: Mike Cole, Rick Young, Dean Pogue, Jerry Hurst, Paul Nazarian, and Wayne Eberly.

In those years, I was welcomed to the pulpits and lecterns of White Memorial Presbyterian Church in Raleigh, North Carolina;

the Mo Ranch Men's Conferences in Hunt, Texas; First Presbyterian Church, Houston; and the Presbytery of St. Augustine leaders' retreat, where I shared summaries of these ideas and took notes of the responses—many of which are reflected in the final content. While in St. Augustine, pastor Cindy Benz and presbytery executive Steve Benz engaged the topic with me at length. One of my newer friends, Brian McLaren, has affirmed the vision for this work.

More recently, I was invited to deliver the Westerveldt Lectures at the Austin Presbyterian Theological Seminary 2015 MidWinter Lectures, where president Theodore Wardlaw, theology professor Dr. Cindy Rigby, and ethics professor Bill Greenway hosted me and offered a few suggestions. All three of them urged me to finish the book and get it published as soon as possible.

In the midst of all of these discussions and events, I dug into some of the great works in ethics: from Dietrich Bonhoeffer to Emil Brunner, from H. Richard Niebuhr to Reinhold Niebuhr, from Stanley Hauerwas to Samuel Wells (his *Improvisation: The Drama of Christian Ethics* is a scholarly treatment that largely converges with mine). I also studied more popular writing on related topics from pastor Adam Hamilton (*Seeing Gray in a Black and White World*) and Garry Friesen (*Decision Making and the Will of God*). Of all of these works, just a few are quoted, but all were fresh in mind as I wrote.

In late 2014, the great folks at Vanderbilt Presbyterian Church, Naples, Florida, welcomed me as their pastor. Soon I was walking three different weekly Bible study classes chapter by chapter through the ideas presented here. Their feedback generated many refinements to the text.

When it came to the final working of the manuscript, my brilliant nephew Scott Doty suggested pertinent anecdotes; Jo Rist did great editing; and editor David Maxwell at Westminster John Knox Press offered many, many suggestions for improvement.

Now, do not presume that all of the above agree with the conclusions offered here. Many will question me; some will argue with me. I take sole responsibility for the content presented.

Above and beyond all of these mentors, guides, critics, and conversation partners, three stand out above all. Son David and daughter Kelly have provided the laboratory of love and learning in which my kernel ideas grew to maturity. My beloved wife, Barbie, added all the more to that lab. Indeed, over the past year, she not only put up with the crazy, busy schedule that accompanied my return to the pastorate but also supported my using days off and evenings to do all of this writing. What's more, she was proofreader *numero uno*; she caught many typos and did it all with grace, raising great questions of what I was saying and how I was saying it so that I would be stating clearly what she knew in her heart to be in my heart. I am so grateful.

Introduction

"The Bible says it. I believe it. That settles it." Or does it? Did it ever? Whenever I see that bumper sticker on a car I sigh a wistful sigh. In fact, I nod in agreement. But my second thought goes more like, "If only. . . ." There was a time when I thought faith was that simple. But then life happened. It got complicated. And when I learned more about what the Bible says, it became apparent that faith wasn't even that simple for those in the Bible!

Oh, I still believe the Bible. I believe that God inspired its writing. But that is one big book. If God needed that many pages to guide our daily living, perhaps God was clueing us in to the fact that life just isn't as simple as the bumper sticker claims.

Yet, God did give us such a book. God knew you and I do want to find answers that stand the test of time. We want those answers because we want to be good and we want to do good. We want to do God's will. "Thy will be done on earth as it is in heaven": More than a few times a week I repeat this line of the Lord's Prayer. Often, amid a crowd of worshipers, I get caught up in the rhythm of familiar words so ingrained in my brain I can say them without thinking. But when I've lingered on this simple appeal, it has made me wonder, "How do I know what God's will is?"

Discerning God's will and following it is complicated. Most of us don't like that. We prefer preachers and prophets who give us simple answers for doing good. We want that bumper sticker to be true. But life just isn't simple. From planning our daily hour-by-hour schedule to wrestling with the biggest controversies around public policy, from choosing a major in college to choosing a mate for life, making good decisions, the kinds of decisions that will actually align our will with that of our loving God, is complicated. It takes hard work.

That's what this book is about.

Pg-13

I invite you to dig into this subject of faithful decision making. But I must warn you. This is not a children's book. If the publisher would label it like the movie industry does, it would require a "Parental Advisory" sticker on it. Not that its sexual content will be prurient; nor will violent scenes gush with blood. And you won't find any foul language. It just won't let you get away with childish, simplistic thinking.

Granted, Jesus said that unless you come to him as a child you will not be able to enter his kingdom, but he did not say that you have to remain as a child forever. His kingdom is not inhabited by toddlers alone. And it isn't led by kindergartners.

This book will press you to wrestle with matters of faith and judgment that recognize that complexities, difficulties, and struggles come with the territory. It will pop the bubble of denial, shallowness, and simplistic platitudes that so often masquerade as courageous, principled living. And it will press you to contemplate the good that dwells in your heart and in those with whom you often find yourself at odds.

Good does dwell within us. In fact, from "good morning" to "good night," our days pulsate with yearnings for a goodness that dwells in the farthest reaches of our most heroic dreams.

The Best Intentions

We humans want to be good. In fact, the aspiration toward goodness is so pervasive that in his book *Mere Christianity* C. S. Lewis cites the existence of human conscience as proof positive of a transcendent divinity.[1] Our consciences demand so much of us and call such

1. C. S. Lewis, *Mere Christianity* (New York: Macmillan Publishing Co., Inc., 1952), 31–35.

good out of us that they could have resulted only from the imprint of an eternally holy Creator, suggests Lewis. They serve as a DNA marker for our having been created in God's own image.

Persons who self-identify as followers of Jesus also testify to a growing desire for goodness sparked by their profession of faith. Jesus said to his disciples, "If you love me, you will keep my commandments" (John 14:15). For good reason. Any person loving another will seek to please that other one. Anybody loving Jesus will seek both to follow his teachings and to emulate his character.

The apostle Paul testifies that "all of us, with unveiled faces, seeing the glory of the Lord as though reflected in a mirror, are being transformed into the same image from one degree of glory to another; for this comes from the Lord, the Spirit" (2 Cor. 3:18). This, he says, serves the ultimate purpose that Jesus would "be the firstborn within a large family" who are "conformed to the image of his Son" (Rom. 8:29).

This process was anticipated by the prophet Jeremiah, who foresaw the day when God would institute a new covenant with the family of God: "I will put my law within them, and I will write it on their hearts; and I will be their God, and they shall be my people" (Jer. 31:33b). That promise is cited word for word by the writer of the book of Hebrews (8:10) as having been initiated in the new covenant established by Jesus Christ and applied by the indwelling presence of the Holy Spirit. Accordingly, in his letter to the Philippians, Paul urges the believers to "work out your own salvation," assured that "it is God who is at work in you, enabling you both to will and to work for his good pleasure" (Phil. 2:12b, 13).

The Devil Is in the DNA

But we're not all sweetness and goodness. Another principle also thrives in the bowels of our beings: the love of the bad. In the 1990s, bad became the new good. Oh, it was one thing to say to a friend, "You look really good." But that compliment paled into nothingness in comparison to the far greater compliment: "You look really bad." That became the ultimate form of flattery. Michael Jackson's song and album *Bad*—which sold something like 879 gazillion copies— tapped into that part of our being that likes to color outside the lines, to light fireworks, to eat indulgent sweets and fatty meats, to drive above the speed limit, to read novels or watch movies that appeal to our naughty side, our sinful inclinations.

Yes, I used that word *sinful*. Jews, Christians, and Muslims alike trace the practice of sin back to a garden in which the first humans were created in the image of God. Then after violating that image, humanity was banished to a life of exile beyond the garden gates. Nevertheless, God still authorized the humans to play God. God stood by the original commission that the humans should create additional humans in their own image. Those children would now be the first mixed-breed humans: created in the image of the holy God and procreated in the image of their sinful human parents—and of their parents' parents, and their parents' parents' parents, and so on.

As if that were not enough, the trinity of negative influences—the world around, the appetites within, and the powers and principalities prowling about—all push and pull, seduce and incite us to expand the breadth and depth of our waywardness.

Cauldrons

Add those negative influences to the yearning for goodness, and we all find within ourselves cauldrons of conflicted desires. The accounts of humanness so vividly portrayed in the unfolding biblical drama of the people of God catch real individuals at their best and at their very worst. One extends pardon to the brothers that sold him into slavery and incarceration. Another musters the courage to believe that with God's help he can topple a giant with a few smooth stones. An army crushes evil empires, routing enemy armies simply by lifting their voices in worshipful song. A stranger finds the strength to help Jesus carry his cross.

The biblical accounts catch those same humans trading their birth-rights for a bowl of soup. They conjure schemes of self-promotion. They sink into the quicksand of their lust. They refuse to apologize and decline to forgive. They showcase an outward generosity to cam-ouflage their miserliness.

This existential ambivalence threw the welcome baby party in the little town of Bethlehem. There, the young virgin writhed in labor while smelling the donkeys' excrement. There, the angel chorus sang in a perfect harmony that the shepherds probably didn't match. And while the star pierced the darkness, it did not pulverize it; night was still night after all. Three-plus decades later, Jesus' death did the opposite: the darkness that eclipsed all hope disintegrated when he burst forth in resurrection light.

By that death and resurrection, Jesus bestowed the gift of forgiveness and reconciliation between humans and their Creator. He granted the gift of righteousness, that is, a right relationship to the holy God. And he initiated a process of changing the lives of all believers by way of sanctifying them, gradually strengthening their true selves—created in God's image—and weakening the grip that their former Godlessness had upon them.

But Then What?

If the grip of badness is loosening its power over believers, how should they then live? The traditional Sunday school response to that question has been, "Follow the Ten Commandments." From Roman Catholics' enumerating sins mortal and venial, to Dutch Reformers printing the Decalogue (lit., "ten words") on the front walls of their sanctuaries, those stone tablets have provided the focal point for civilizations' moral and ethical codes for three millennia.

But we have a problem with the commandments beyond that of our own weakened willpower to follow them. An even bigger problem looms in the hairline fractures that peel through our brains: we don't really and truly believe in those commandments in the way most of us claim.

The Troublesome Ten

A funny thing happens on the way to following the commandments of God: we trip over them.

- We're commanded by Moses to disassociate from false gods, and in the New Testament the apostles (Acts 15) forbid eating food offered to idols. But then the apostle Paul tells the Corinthians to go ahead and eat whatever food their pagan neighbors serve, in effect saying, "Don't ask. Don't tell."

- We're commanded to keep the Sabbath holy—doing no work—yet on one of those days Jesus allows his disciples, while walking through farmland, to harvest, husk, and eat grain just because they didn't want to wait till sundown.
- We're told to honor our parents, but when a man called by Jesus to follow him responds, "'First let me go and bury my father.' Jesus shuns him, saying, "'Let the dead bury their own dead'" (Luke 9:60). And on another occasion he says,

"Do not think that I have come to bring peace to the earth; I have not come to bring peace, but a sword.

For I have come to set a man against his father,
and a daughter against her mother,
and a daughter-in-law against her mother-in-law;
and one's foes will be members of one's own household.

Whoever loves father or mother more than me is not worthy of me; and whoever loves son or daughter more than me is not worthy of me."

(Matt. 10:34–37)

- We're told not to bear false witness, but given the option between offending with the truth and peace making with a white lie, we'll choose the latter at least once in a while.

You name a major commandment in the Bible, and you probably can find a story in the Bible wherein a hallowed superstar violates that very command—and does so with impunity or even with endorsement.

Battling Believers

What's more, followers of Jesus are not exactly of one mind on all matters of morals and ethics. In the present era the loudest debates have revolved around matters of same-gender attraction and relationships. Should the twenty-first-century church be excluding gay, lesbian, bisexual, and transgendered (LGBT) expressions of sexual intimacy as it has through past millennia? Or should the church embrace those of the LGBT community and even consecrate same-gender unions and marriages with the same wonder and joy as surround traditional opposite-gender marriages?

Just about as loud are the internecine battles over life-and-death matters, especially abortion. Should the conception of a child within a womb be celebrated always as a miracle and that fetus be granted protected status? Or should the mother be entrusted with the authority to choose whether to carry to term or to abort that fetus? What about those tragic situations of pregnancies caused by incest or rape, and of medical threats to the mother's own life? What about end-of-life situations, the painful questions surrounding the sustaining of a body via extraordinary measures? And is the death penalty an appropriate application of divine justice or a wretched venting of human vengeance?

What about a citizen's duty to support the environment? And should Christians support and defend Israel—speaking out on behalf of the Jews—Jesus' birth family? Or should Christians support and defend Palestinians, among whom are a significant number of Christians? And what does it look like to be Christian peacemakers in that troubled land? Or, indeed, should both people-groups be held to the same kinds of international laws and standards as other noniconic peoples? And are women and men equals in all respects, or should they be complementary partners with distinct roles to fulfill?

Every major monotheist faith—Jewish, Christian, Muslim—suffers innumerable internal disputes over conflicting viewpoints held by people of intense faith whose ideological passion is prompted by a yearning to be right and good.

Other Nagging Questions

Apart from the hotly debated controversies, humans of all stripes face age-old questions whose answers continually elude simple explanation:

- How to manage personal finances
- With whom to endeavor to build a life together as family
- How to cope with addictions—one's own and another's
- How to choose a career

This book can't thoroughly tackle all of these topics. But the nagging nature of all of them prompts me to ask in a broad, sweeping way, "How can we know what God would have us to do in such complicated times? Furthermore, can our understanding of God's guidance lead to the kind of empowerment that would actually help us to achieve the better good toward which our best selves aspire?"

Another Book?

What can this book offer to help address such matters? What is my plan? First, I will pull together several kinds of questions into a single framework. Books on morals and ethics abound. Books on discerning one's vocation or calling abound (both secular-vocation books and religious-calling books). Books on understanding God's will for everyday questions abound. This book will tackle all of those questions at once because they are all related. It will tackle practical life questions while keeping sweeping ethical concerns in view. I'll be wearing my priestly alb, my professorial tweed jacket, and my guidance-counselor open-collar shirt all at once.

Second, I will take you on a journey through the Bible to encounter both sweeping themes and the idiosyncratic oddities that seem to defy them. Together we will seek to understand God's will as revealed by Spirit-inspired writers who were dealing themselves in the toughest decisions of their lives in the complicated times of their lives. We will listen intently to Jesus, and we'll watch to see how his disciples interpreted and implemented his mission in foreign lands and divergent cultures long after his ascension took his audible voice away from them. Instead of shushing to silence the Scripture passages that don't match our Sunday school training, we'll embrace them, consider them, and help make sense of them. In the process, we will treat every page of the Bible as inspired by God.

Third, I will help you formulate an interpretive framework for addressing your questions in the light of such biblical teachings. In lectures preparatory to writing this book, I kiddingly have spoken about "doing ethics by spreadsheet." Well, all kidding aside, I will lay out for you four different spreadsheets that will form a logical and faithful way to interpret the Scriptures to be applied to your life. And while you won't be carrying such spreadsheets in your pockets any more than were Mary, John, Peter, or Paul, hopefully the framework will stick with you to equip you to discern your way through these complicated times.

In the process I will aim to affirm your best intentions, giving language to the learnings that your experiences, study, and intuition all have built into your heart and mind. And, hopefully, you'll be equipped to help others to do the same.

Have you ever watched the on-field interview of the game's most valuable player at a Super Bowl, which is usually the winning team's quarterback? The sportscaster typically asks a simple question: "What was your key to such success?" Typically, the sweaty, exhilarated athlete says something like "It was all about the offensive line. Those guys gave me the time to throw. They opened holes for the running backs. They were just spectacular." No doubt those normally unsung, little-noticed linemen deserve credit and appreciate being singled out like that, but, truth be told, there are a lot of other reasons for the team's success:

- The heroic pass catching of the wide receivers
- The speedy ball carrying of the running backs
- The stifling defensive play that went on while that quarterback was sitting on the bench
- The brilliant coaching coming from the sidelines
- The encyclopedic research prepared in advance by the teams' scouts
- The savvy trades made by the team's coaches in the off-season
- The millions of dollars invested by the team's owner to put all that talent together on one team

Christian decision making usually gets explained in simple categories and simplistic, reductionist logic. In reality, however, it operates in complex, intricate, overlapping, and ambiguous ways. Most of us make good decisions much of the time, but like the victorious quarterback, we explain our decision-making processes to our friends and children in ways that don't actually match how we really made those decisions. We don't know how to preach what we practice.

In a Nutshell

This book hopes to help you, the reader, to think through your practices and to figure out how to tell others the same. To preach what, indeed, you practice. Specifically, my goal is to help you articulate an authentically Christian way of discerning God's will for your personal life decisions (both the big ones and the small ones) and for your life together with others in Christian community—indeed, in the whole kingdom of God.

By *authentically* I mean "honestly": not claiming to be something or someone that you are not; not pretending to others or yourself that things are better or worse than they really are; not discounting your own character nor exaggerating your own culpability; and not pretending that God makes all stories have happy endings. To be authentic is to be genuine, true, and transparent.

By *Christian way of discerning God's will*, I do not exclude the Jewish and Muslim way of discerning God's will. However, this book will specifically tap the principles taught and modeled in both the Hebrew Bible or Christian Old Testament and in the Christian New Testament, treating those two sets of documents as the Word of God. The whole Bible will be our textbook, taking seriously not only the clear, definitive commands found therein but also the vague, confusing, odd commands and incidents reported as well. I will show how the Bible itself gives us clues on how to integrate the points of inconsistency and ambiguity.

Your search to learn how to *discern God's will for your personal life and for your life together with others* will hold those two realms together. We won't allow our American individualism to eclipse our life in community. We won't allow community goals and needs to trample over individual rights and responsibilities. And the community we will address will include not only your nuclear family and local congregation but also the larger church of the denominational and ecumenical world. It will even include the kingdom of God that was first glimpsed four thousand years ago when a man and woman were told to leave their homeland to go to a place prepared for them. This is the God thing that God is doing in the world—proceeding toward the day when all can say that the kingdoms of this world have become the kingdom of our Lord and Christ, just as he taught us to pray, "Thy kingdom come, thy will be done on earth as in heaven."

Ultimately, my hope is that we together will discover a truly ethical way of living, will actualize maturity in Christ, and will show forth a witness of authenticity and candor that bring credit to the faith and that cause our lives to sing a new song of joy. You see, what's so great about being good is that the grace of the Lord Jesus Christ, unleashed on the world by the love of God, makes possible the experience of communing together in the fellowship of the Holy Spirit. And the Spirit's power has been unleashed in us to teach and to empower us to desire and to actually implement the Lord's work in the world.

But what about the will of God? How might we discern it? How can we know and live the greater good? Let us together seek faithful answers to these questions in order to help us make faithful decisions all toward the end of living faithful lives.

1

Searching for Certitude

An oft-told story about the late Bishop Fulton Sheen references a sidewalk conversation he had with a young boy. Sheen was scheduled to speak in Philadelphia at town hall. He decided to walk there from his hotel even though he was unfamiliar with the city. Sure enough, he got lost and was forced to ask some boys to direct him to his destination.

One of them asked Sheen, "What are you doing there?"

"I'm going to give a lecture," said the bishop.

"About what?"

"On how to get to heaven. Would you care to come along?"

"Are you kidding?" said the boy. "You don't even know how to get to town hall." In today's world, Sheen could have found his way by pulling out his smartphone and telling it where he wanted to end up, and it would have guided his every step. But most of life's decisions have not been simplified by twenty-first-century technologies.

Two Questions

We still are pressed to answer two questions: What is the right thing to do? And how can you know for sure? Those two questions have commanded the attention of persons from the beginning of time.

Some have applied themselves to intense academic study of ethics to find out. Others have sought the counsel of astrologers or Tarot card readers. Some have traveled the high seas to find a wise guide. Others have leaned on the charismata of knowledge, discernment, and wisdom. Many have read their respective holy book(s). More than anything, Christians have looked to the Bible to guide them.

The language used across the spectrum of Christian traditions ranges widely. Some seek "God's perfect will" while accepting "God's permissive will." Others participate in discernment groups. Some testify, "God is leading me to. . . ." Others say, "I am following God's call on my life." What they all hold in common is the confidence that God really does have a plan, a specific purpose for their lives. Some pursue such insights expecting open-ended options. They will pray for God to open their eyes to see what God intends for them, but they won't sit around waiting for lightning to strike. Others expect a custom-designed plan to guide them. They heard along the way, "God loves you and has a wonderful plan for your life." So they watch and pray for that plan to appear like the handwriting on the wall or, in more modern terms, as directions drawn on a Google Maps site. Others are willing to take it one turn at a time, as in a GPS navigation system in the car.

One Perfect Plan?

How awesome is it to think that God has a specific plan for your life? The prospect of that sounds compelling. *Wow, the almighty, transcendent God of the universe has singled me out for something big to do!* How dignifying that is. Such a claim seems to match the affirmation of Jeremiah: "For surely I know the plans I have for you, says the LORD, plans for your welfare and not for harm, to give you a future with hope" (Jer. 29:11).

But was Jeremiah intending that promise for you in particular? As a matter of fact, the promise was expressed to a plurality of persons. The word of assurance was proclaimed to the people of Israel, akin to something a president may promise to the nation as a whole. Does it mean, "I have a specific plan for each and every one of you, down to the finest detail of every decision each one will ever make?"

When speaking of God's good plan for our lives, we generally turn the promise into our hopes for our own lives and those of our loved ones. Surely, we reason, just as Jesus promised to prepare a place in heaven for us to enjoy our eternal rest, so too he has promised to lead us to the perfect church, the perfect set of friends, the perfect college and major to study, the perfect career, the perfect spouse.

Success seems to stand just one set of instructions away from the moment. If only we could order directions like a three-course meal from a menu, then God's plan for our lives would begin to play itself out perfectly. In effect, this model of guidance is conditioned simply on the assignment to follow directions. The transcendent global-positioning-satellite reader guides you every step of the way. Churches of all kinds of stripes have been broadcasting this set of promises for decades.

But in 1988, Garry Friesen, a professor at Multnomah Bible College in Portland, Oregon, turned that thinking on its ear. His book *Decision Making and the Will of God: A Biblical Alternative to the Traditional View* dismantled the road-map model of discerning God's will. As Friesen outlines it, the traditional approach takes literally the modern evangelists' promise "God has a wonderful plan for your life," which, he claims, has turned the Christian journey into a treasure hunt—with the sure promise that if only you can decipher the particular plan designed for your life, all will go well with you.

Friesen characterizes that traditional approach as the search for the "bull's eye" of God's will—knowing that when taking bow and arrow in hand, reaching anything outside the target's perfect center stands as a failure. But what happens when you find what appears to be the bull's eye and the treasure map takes you to that new job to which God called you, but your boss morphs into an arrogant ogre? What does that say about God's wonderful plan for your life? Should you just assume that you missed the bull's eye of God's plan, proceed to quit the job, and, with God's help, find the job your Lord had really intended you to have all along?

Or if you think God has led you to the right spouse but she or he turns into an abusive drug addict, what then? What does that say about God's wonderful plan for your life? Should you just assume and acknowledge that you missed the bull's eye, divorce that person, and, with God's help, find the actual perfect spouse God intended you to have all along? Or should you just try to love that partner into better behavior, pretending to others that you're living in marital bliss—if only to protect God's reputation—thereby being a mere enabler of escalating violence?

Sure, this sounds melodramatic, but too many evils have been perpetuated and enabled by victims protecting others' reputations—including that of their supposedly loving Lord. The search for the bull's eye too often leads to miles and piles of troubles. Such a search often leads to irresponsible behavior by the believer at hand. If life's successes result from being in the right place, then being the energetic worker or loving spouse or caring parent or studious professor or script-memorizing actor or attentive police officer gets short shrift. In the real world, success has more to do with what you do than with where you are.

Baggage

The God's-wonderful-plan notion, attractive as it sounds, carries so much baggage that it's almost nonsensical. For one thing, few believers actually order their lives according to it. Sure, when facing really major decisions, like whom to marry, many an earnest believer will pray for God's will to be made clear. They may even see if the "channel markers" align—circumstances, inner witness, wise counsel from others, personal desires, common sense, and special guidance—to give a clear answer to their prayerful questioning. However, even earnest, God-honoring adherents make moment-by-moment decisions about matters of monumental significance—like changing lanes on a highway—without exploring any of these guidance systems.

For another thing, this bull's-eye approach breeds a dangerous subjectivity. Its God-centered talk actually disguises its self-centered mentality: "What is God's plan for my life?" implies, oh, so subtly, that God exists for me. Such self-absorption can foster eccentric actions and emotionalism—where feelings trump good judgment, intelligence, and analysis. It sometimes leads to one superspiritual person outshouting another.

Imagine yourself being the parent of a young-adult son who begins his morning every day by calling you on the phone: "Mom, just checking in to see what I should be doing today. What should I do?" In all likelihood, you'd tell your son to get out of bed and get to school or work. Or you'd tell him to call his therapist. Or worse, you would have him committed to a psychiatric hospital.

We don't think of mature adults as people who are simply waiting to be given orders for their day. Even basic training—that military process that establishes a bottom line of taking orders—quickly moves recruits from blind obedience to the formation of the kind of character that can make wise decisions moment-by-moment in the most harrowing of situations. Would our loving sovereign Parent expect us to be imbeciles?

One other bit of bull's-eye baggage is its tendency to turn the Christian journey into one of endless searching for special knowledge, a kind of enlightenment. The ancient Christians dubbed this Gnosticism. They called it a heresy. Drawn from the Greek word *gnosko* literally, "to know," the gnostics searched endlessly for—and sometimes claimed to have received—a kind of knowledge that was kept for them alone, one not shared with average, pedestrian people.

Gnosticism flies in the face of the good news of the self-disclosing God. From the first conversations with humans in Eden to the incarnation of God's Son in Bethlehem, from the delivery of the Ten Commandments to Moses to the revelation recorded by the apostle John, God's will is not shrouded in mystery to be doled out piecemeal by soothsayers or mountain mystics. God's will has been made known by the Word-made-flesh, as conveyed in the written word.

Gnosticism also misses the fact that Christian living is built on the grace of God embraced via trust, not on the mysteries of God caught via mystical insight. It is a religion consisting essentially of faith in action, not ideas in contemplation.

Ultimately, the bull's-eye model simply misses the Bible's call to grow in wisdom. If, as is often said, wisdom is "applied knowledge," then people of wisdom are students of all kinds of understanding, analysts of life's lessons, practitioners of good judgment, masters of common sense, and followers of the will and ways of God that have been made known in God's word. These believers have learned a different way to understand and apply God's will and ways because they have learned to change the question.

Changing the Question

If those subscribing to the bull's-eye model of discernment repeatedly ask, "What is God's perfect plan for my life," then people of wisdom ask, "How might I make a godly decision about what

I should do?" This alternative question presumes that the person already enjoys at least a basic level of knowledge. Indeed, the words from Micah 6:8 that say we are required to do justice, love mercy, and walk humbly with our God begin with the summary statement "He has told you, O mortal, what is good." As the voice of conscience tells us, we don't need a prophetic utterance to know that some behaviors are obligatory, some advisable, some dangerous, and others unconscionable.

This question implicitly acknowledges that ours is a multiple-choice world. We aren't offered just one right option—God's perfect will—amid a sea of monstrous alternatives. In fact, many choices do not pose moral dilemmas. Many, if not most, simply require us to choose one good option from among many possibilities.

This new question also lends itself to a great invention: the midcourse correction. Watch any competitive sporting event. If one strategy doesn't score the goal, then the coach sends in another. If the pitcher keeps walking the batters, a relief pitcher is brought to the mound.

To ask, "How might I make a godly decision about what I should do?" allows a person to postulate multiple strategies, to glean elements from one, mix them with another one or two or more, continue exploring questions while experimenting with possible answers, and making adjustments at every point along the way.

Even more importantly, this question invites us to take responsibility for our actions rather than put all of the initiative and therefore both credit and blame for the results on God. And yes, sometimes things go wrong because we made a bad judgment call. Sometimes we fail because we violated what we knew we should do. Sometimes things go badly because somebody else made a mistake. And sometimes bad things do happen to good people.

The Mind of Christ

Asking ourselves how we can make godly decisions presses us to be good students of God's word and will. Building on what we said above about knowing God's will does not mean that we always know it on our own. The search for wisdom challenges us to do our research, to become conversant with God's word.

Quoting from the prophet Isaiah, the apostle Paul asks, "'Who has known the mind of the Lord so as to instruct him?'" He answers simply. "But we have the mind of Christ" (1 Cor. 2:16). Most of us, however, have the mind of the Screen Writers Guild. Or of a particular brand of broadcast journalism. Or of a political party. Or of our family roots. Biblical prophets heard multiple voices and influences, but they did aim to be shaped by God's word:

> Your words were found, and I ate them,
>   and your words became to me a joy
>   and the delight of my heart;
> for I am called by your name,
>   O LORD, God of hosts.
>   (Jer. 15:16)

> The law of the LORD is perfect,
>   reviving the soul;
> the decrees of the LORD are sure,
>   making wise the simple;
> the precepts of the LORD are right,
>   rejoicing the heart;
> the commandment of the LORD is clear,
>   enlightening the eyes;
> the fear of the LORD is pure,
>   enduring forever;
> the ordinances of the LORD are true
>   and righteous altogether.
> More to be desired are they than gold,
>   even much fine gold;
> sweeter also than honey,
>   and drippings of the honeycomb.
>   (Ps. 19:7–10)

> All scripture is inspired by God and is useful for teaching, for reproof, for correction, and for training in righteousness, so that everyone who belongs to God may be proficient, equipped for every good work. (2 Tim. 3:16–17)

These writers' reflections span hundreds of years, but they all share in common a love for, an appetite to ingest, and an ongoing pattern of analyzing, studying, and seeking to apply God's self-revelation. They trusted that most of what they needed to know had been taught them in the Holy Scriptures, and they were applying themselves to see God's words unfold before, around, and within them.

Discernment?

So what about your discernment? That very word has become one of the most widely used buzzwords of the early twenty-first century in spirituality circles. Still, the term *discernment* often echoes the "bull's eye" mind-set outlined above. Many of its proponents seem to suggest that the search for a certain path and destination can be ascertained before taking the first step. It also suggests that once decided, one need make no course corrections or even adjustments along the way, but life just does not work that way. Sometimes one's step out into the unknown will feel like the appropriate response to a perceived prod from providential directional signals, but the mature, adult Christian will make numerous adjustments along the way. Wisdom requires that.

If we are going to take our language seriously, then we need to acknowledge that the biblical word *discernment* is used exclusively to speak of spiritual insight to assess the origin of an idea, an attitude, or behavior. Does it come from God or from the forces of evil? In fact, "discernment of the spirits" (1 Cor. 12:10) correlates with the exorcising of demons as practiced by Jesus and the apostles. Or, as specifically declared in 1 Cor. 2:14, "the person without the Spirit does not accept the things that come from the Spirit of God but considers them foolishness, and cannot understand them because they are discerned only through the Spirit." That hardly matches the simple act of asking God for guidance envisioned by regular Christian folk.

What is needed for believers is not a singular strategy to discover the one right thing God has planned but the cultivation of the kind of wisdom with which one can make godly decisions about what one should do. What one needs is to so imbibe the mind of Christ as revealed in Scripture that one can be conversant with and attentive to the guidance provided by the revealed words of God. Of course, actually learning God's will through the reading of the Bible is more easily said than done. That book is complicated, just as life is complicated. We will need to take a closer look at the holy writ of Scripture to see what insights it can give us. We turn to that subject in the next chapter.

2

The Troubling Ten

"Do you accept the books of the Old and New Testaments to be, by God's inspiration, the unique and authoritative witness to Jesus Christ and God's word to you?" Any person preparing to be ordained and/or installed into service within my denomination is asked this question. In order to qualify, the candidate must respond, "I do." Similar questions are asked of those being ordained in many, if not most, other denominations.

In each of the several times I have been asked this question, I have earnestly answered, "I do." But herein lies a problem. In order for the Bible to operate as God's word to me I have to read it receptively and with an eye toward obeying it, yet on many counts and in many places it gets really confusing, ambiguous, and self-contradictory. To people who, like me, hold the Bible in the highest esteem as God's word to the world and to themselves, this chapter will throw some difficult curves. Or, to be more exact, it will bat back to the Bible curves that the Bible actually throws at sincere students of the Book. This may be discombobulating for you. It may shock you. It may cause you to throw up your hands in dismay.

But do not despair. As the one who compiled the data to be presented, I still heartily affirm that vow taken at my ordination—to accept the books of the Bible as God's authoritative witness. I want to assure you that the challenges being tossed out in this chapter will find substantive answers in subsequent chapters.

Not that this affirmation is made glibly and with ease. These curves have tested my sensibilities. But I have never lost confidence in the Bible as the words of the living God who so loved the world that he gave his only begotten Son—the living Word—that whosoever believes in him will not perish but have eternal life. In fact, my many wrestling matches over these verses have brought me closer to God and closer to a deeper appreciation for and trust in the written Word of God. It is the fully inspired, fully authoritative, holy Bible.

Still, it would be a good idea to put on your seat belt. We are going on a wild ride.

The Recuperating Fourth

Here is the problem. Some of the commands expressed most pointedly and demandingly in some parts of the Bible seem to get shrugged off in other parts of the Bible. Take, for example, the Ten Commandments (aka the Decalogue). Consider the Fourth Commandment: "Remember the sabbath day, and keep it holy" (Exod. 20:8), which Exodus 31:14–15 elaborates:

> "You shall keep the Sabbath, because it is holy to you; everyone who profanes it shall be put to death; whoever does any work on it shall be cut off from among the people. Six days shall work be done, but the seventh day is a sabbath of solemn rest, holy to the LORD; whoever does any work on the sabbath day shall be put to death."

Those are threatening words.

On the other hand, Matthew tells of an occasion in which Jesus allowed his disciples to work on the Sabbath.

> At that time Jesus went through the grainfields on the sabbath; his disciples were hungry, and they began to pluck heads of grain and to eat. When the Pharisees saw it, they

said to him, "Look! Your disciples are doing what it is not lawful to do on the sabbath." (Matt. 12:1–3)

Jesus defended the apostles' work by retelling an obscure story from the life of David.

> He said to them, "Have you not read what David did when he and his companions were hungry? He entered the house of God and ate the bread of the Presence, which it was not lawful for him or his companions to eat, but only for the priests. Or have you not read in the law that on the sabbath the priests in the temple break the Sabbath and yet are guiltless? I tell you, something greater than the temple is here. But if you had known what this means, 'I desire mercy and not sacrifice,' you would not have condemned the guiltless. For the Son of Man is lord of the sabbath." (12:4–8)

Then, Jesus leverages his reasoning to justify performing a miracle on the Sabbath.

Now mind you, it's one thing for Jesus to heal the sick on the Sabbath. The sick need medical support seven days of the week. But plucking grain? That's work. Physical labor. Given that the Sabbath begins with sundown on Friday and ends with sundown on Saturday, could not the disciples have waited till dark to glean some grain from one of the fields? Were their grumbling stomachs a disease unto death?

Then again, when Paul later took up the topic in his letter to the Romans, he relativizes the whole subject (Rom. 14:5): "Some judge one day to be better than another, while others judge all days to be alike. Let all be fully convinced in their own minds." That final sentence is especially telling. The Old Testament book of Judges ends with a summary judgment upon the whole era: "In those days there was no king in Israel; all the people did what was right in their own eyes" (Judg. 21:25). Paul expresses this same idea not with approbation but with approval.

At very least, the commands to keep the Sabbath and the corresponding death threats to those not subscribing to them appear to be less than absolute.

The Troubling Ninth

Consider another "absolute," the Ninth Commandment: "You shall not bear false witness against your neighbor" (Exod. 20:16). This prohibition is echoed—along with a threat for noncompliance—in Proverbs 19:5: "A false witness will not go unpunished, and a liar will not escape." But what about the deceptions of Jacob that stole from his older brother Esau the family blessing normally conveyed upon the firstborn? Did Jacob perish? Did he suffer even the slightest punishment? What about the lies the prostitute Rahab told to the civil authorities to protect the Jewish spies who were hiding in her home? Not only was she saved by her deceptions, but she was also commended for her faith centuries later by the writer of the book of Hebrews (11:31).

Worse than all of these, Jesus himself actually commends dishonest business practices:

> Then Jesus said to the disciples, "There was a rich man who had a manager, and charges were brought to him that this man was squandering his property. So he summoned him and said to him, 'What is this that I hear about you? Give me an accounting of your management, because you cannot be my manager any longer.' Then the manager said to himself, 'What will I do, now that my master is taking the position away from me? I am not strong enough to dig, and I am ashamed to beg. I have decided what to do so that, when I am dismissed as manager, people may welcome me into their homes.' So, summoning his master's debtors one by one, he asked the first, 'How much do you owe my master?' He answered, 'A hundred jugs of olive oil.' He said to him, 'Take your bill, sit down quickly, and make it fifty.' Then he asked another, 'And how much do you owe?' He replied, 'A hundred containers of wheat.' He said to him, 'Take your bill and make it eighty.' And his master commended the dishonest manager because he had acted shrewdly; for the children of this age are more shrewd in dealing with their own generation than are the children of light. And I tell you, make friends for yourselves by means of dishonest wealth so

that when it is gone, they may welcome you into the eternal
homes. (Luke 16:1–9)

We can certainly justify Jesus' parable on the basis of economic
realities. We can compare it to industry standards of modern-day debt
collectors and agree that Jesus is lifting up an approach of "something
is better than nothing." But if we are going to measure the manager's
actions against the Ten Commandments, they come up short. And
Jesus' specific endorsement of using "means of dishonest wealth" does
not match the explicit meaning of "Thou shalt not bear false witness."

The Covenantal Seventh

Back to the story of Rahab and the Israeli spies (Josh. 2:1–21; 6:17–
25). Lest we rush by that story, we cannot overlook the fact that it
throws a curve or two at the "absolute" Seventh Commandment:
"You shall not commit adultery" (Exod. 20:14). She who enjoyed
the favor of the invading Israelites curried that favor by being a pro-
fessional adulterer. Amazingly, the book of Hebrews not only commends her faith as one who welcomed the Israeli spies but even
identifies her as "Rahab the prostitute" (Heb. 11:31). What's so com-
mendable about prostitutes welcoming strangers? How else do they
earn their living? The writers of Joshua and Hebrews both seem to
take the Seventh Commandment somewhat lightly.

Speaking of that commandment, what are we to do with the reports
of polygamous kings in Judea and Israel—the most extreme being King
Solomon, who had seven hundred wives and three hundred concu-
bines (1 Kgs. 11:3)? Less extreme in number but shocking in initiative
are King David's covenants with eight wives. Never to be forgotten is
the judgment incurred by David for arranging the slaying of Uriah,
carried out so that he could arrange to take Bathsheba as his own wife.
The wickedness of the one God called "a man after his own heart" (1
Sam. 13:14) was confronted by the prophet Nathan. The prophet did
not mince words either in the substance or in the attribution of origin:

> Thus says the LORD, the God of Israel: I anointed you king
> over Israel, and I rescued you from the hand of Saul; I gave
> you your master's house, and your master's wives into your

bosom, and gave you the house of Israel and of Judah; and if that had been too little, I would have added as much more. Why have you despised the word of the LORD, to do what is evil in his sight? You have struck down Uriah the Hittite with the sword, and have taken his wife to be your wife, and have killed him with the sword of the Ammonites. (2 Sam. 12:7–9)

Did you catch the stunner in the words? According to Nathan, God turned Saul's multiple wives over to David to be joined to him (i.e., "into your bosom"). So the taking of multiple wives, while indulged somewhat as typical of royals in the ancient world was initiated in this instance not by an international peace treaty but directly by God. Whatever happened to the Seventh Commandment?

The Respectful Fifth Commandment

Then again, what happened to the "absolute" Fifth Commandment? "Honor your father and your mother, so that your days may be long in the land that the LORD your God is giving you" (Exod. 20:12; cf., Deut. 5:18). Like other commandments, this commandment carries sanctions against violators: "Whoever curses father or mother shall be put to death" (Exod. 21:17). Jesus affirms the importance of following this commandment in the process of scolding Pharisees for devising strategies to permit disobedience of parents (Matt. 15:3–8; Mark 7:9–13), and the letter to the Ephesians reaffirms it as "the first commandment with a promise" (6:2).

Still, into this consensus Jesus drives a wedge of dissent:

"Do not think that I have come to bring peace to the earth; I have not come to bring peace, but a sword.

> For I have come to set a man against his father,
> and a daughter against her mother,
> and a daughter-in-law against her mother-in-law;
> and one's foes will be members of one's own household.

Whoever loves father or mother more than me is not worthy of me; and whoever loves son or daughter more than me is not worthy of me; and whoever does not take up the cross and follow me is not worthy of me. Those who find their life will lose it, and those who lose their life for my sake will find it." (Matt. 10:34–39; see also Luke 12:49–53)

Those words, even if interpreted as intentionally hyperbolic, certainly diminish the absolute status of the command to always honor one's parents. So much for the authority of the Fifth Commandment.

What Now?

What are we to make of these contradictions? Is there no guidance from the Bible that we can trust? When facing the facts of what actually is in the Bible, it's easy to react one way or the other. Some who have encountered these apparent contradictions have thrown hands into the air and, in disgust, have simply written off the Bible as nonsense, nothing but a maze of confusion. Some have even pointed a shaming finger back at their pastors, priests, and Sunday school teachers, accusing them (usually in absentia) of lying to them. In the process they have thrown the Bible into the junk heap.

Others faced with these perplexities have simply cupped their hands over their ears and pretended they'd never encountered such aberrations. They keep merrily rolling along in a state of safe denial—holding on to the propositional truths that have safely guided them in the past. They busily fill their minds with reassurances of what they know to be true and hope that the memories of these contradictions will soon fade away.

The Bible and its primary author, God, deserve better than either of these reactions. The sheer range—in time and distances—of the Bible's influence demands that its perplexities be more carefully considered. At the same time, however, the points of departure within the Bible also beg for close consideration. If disparities exist, then those who read the sixty-six books that comprise the big Book owe it to the Bible to take those differences as important.

Could it be that God actually intended those contradictions to exist? If God did not so intend, then their presence begs for some better kind of explanation.

Absolutes?

Each of the above commandments was introduced as an "absolute." The term is used here because so many Christians use it to describe the Ten Commandments along with a handful—maybe even a host—of other commands spelled out in Scripture. But is it the right term to be using?

Consider this: An absolute is an absolute and therefore allows no room for anything less than the absolute. Have you ever used the expression "mostly absolute" or "almost absolute"? Of course not. To be absolute is to be totally yes or totally no. It does not allow for maybe. It's either 100 percent or zero percent. Anything apart from total fails the "absolute" test.

As one well-schooled in biblical apologetics, I could present an almost compelling argument to prove that each of the departures from the commandments is not really what it appears to be. But they wouldn't really satisfy the sincere, inquiring mind. Each one of these cases is, at the very least, a partial departure. Accordingly, they should be labeled sins—including those taught or carried out by Jesus—or the commandments themselves ought to shed the term *absolutes*.

Not willing to countenance the former option, I propose that we simply drop the label. That's not to suggest that there are no absolutes. The existence of God—"I AM that I AM"—is incontrovertible, undebatable, nonnegotiable. It is an absolute. The doctrine of the Holy Trinity is an absolute. Every major ecumenical organization from the National Association of Evangelicals to the World Council of Churches requires every member church to affirm its commitment to the Trinity. The full humanity and divinity of Christ Jesus is an absolute, as is Jesus' work of bringing salvation to the world by his incarnation, his crucifixion—dying for human sin—and his resurrection from the dead. The doctrine of salvation by grace through faith stands as an absolute.

Yes, absolutes do reign supreme at the center of Christian faith. But when it comes to the biblical directives for human behavior, the word *absolute* overstates each and every one. Indeed, basically every command regarding human behavior—whether referred to as ethics, morals, calling, discernment, or the will of God—has a range of movement within and around it. The term *absolutes* just does not apply here.

Anything Goes?

So what are we to say of the Bible's commands? Do the Ten Commandments have any bearing at all? They absolutely do. Just not as absolutes. The key to interpreting, applying, and obeying the biblical teaching on God's will lies in effective reading of the Bible itself. Two essential keys to reading it are as follows:

- Read each text with an eye toward understanding what the original, God-inspired writer was intending the original audience to understand that text to mean.
- Compare all texts relating to the topic against one another to assess the relative gravity, clarity, force, and range of applications that emerge from such comparisons.

The first of the above points is what is best called "intentionality exegesis"; the second has long been dubbed "the analogy of Scripture."

Intentionality exegesis is a fancy way of saying, "Read the Gospel, or the letter, or the historical report, or the poem, or the proverb, or whatever it is, in the way that the original writer intended to be communicating." Just as we read different genres differently, a poem about a beautiful pond versus a chemical analysis of the water in the pond, so too the writings within the Bible convey their thoughts in ways consistent with the genre each original writer chose. Further, each writer was addressing situations particular to the audience to which the writing was addressed, and each writer chose the words, the tenses, the syntactical arrangement of words appropriate to the message to be conveyed.

A serious student of the Scriptures—no matter what bias she or he may have—will need to try to analyze the text, the historical situation, and the flow of ideas in order to best understand the intentions of that writer. When it comes to drawing broad, sweeping guidance from Scripture, one needs to compare all texts that relate to the topic. Some of those texts will address all of the specifics in exactly the same way, and some will offer a variety of directives. Some will tell stories that add color and nuance; some stories may point in angular ways; and some may draw more sweeping, broader perspectives.

When studying Scripture in such ways, one is joining a host of biblical students through the centuries. From the greatest exegetical scholars to the humblest elementary-level Sunday school teachers, these straightforward approaches have yielded insightful and lasting guidance from the Bible. Which takes us back to the question of the Bible's commands. Are they null and void? Absolutely not. They do guide human behavior in ways both definitive and ambiguous, directive and suggestive. Let us dig further to see where that all might go.

3

From Absolutes to Aspirations

S o how shall we read the Bible in a way that helps us to apply it in our present situations and that actually gives constructive guidance? And given that biblical teachings do not specifically serve as absolutes for us, how shall we read the Bible?

My proposal is that we interpret the Bible in ways comparable to how the Bible interprets itself. Time and again New Testament speakers, especially Jesus, and writers such as Paul and the Gospel writers quote from the Old Testament. Perhaps we can follow their example.

Biblical Interpretation

When studying in my seminary, we learned the necessity of doing intentional exegesis, asking, "What was the original writer intending the original readers to understand and do?" We were also taught to compare biblical texts using the "the analogy of Scripture" approach. But Jesus and his biographers seem to take some Old Testament texts in ways that were not consistent with the original writers' intentions, so when fellow seminarians asked our professors why we couldn't do the same, the stock response was "You're not Jesus." And they added, "You're not Matthew or John or Paul either."

It was a fair response, but the professors would add still further, "And you're not inspired by the Holy Spirit to write the Scriptures." Another fair response, but these were not entirely satisfying answers to our original question. Might there still be some lessons in the interpretation and application of the Scriptures resident in the exegetical work of the New Testament writers as they held in their hands the holy words of God presented in the Law, the Prophets, the Psalms, and the Wisdom literature?

A Case Study

An invaluable case study comes to us from the middle of the book of Acts. One commandment of the Old Testament treated as a non-negotiable absolute was given generations prior to the Decalogue. When inviting Abram and Sarai into covenant, God directed Abram to be circumcised and then to do so with all succeeding sons, grandsons, and all male progeny thereafter.

> God said to Abraham, "As for you, you shall keep my covenant, you and your offspring after you throughout their generations. This is my covenant, which you shall keep, between me and you and your offspring after you: Every male among you shall be circumcised. You shall circumcise the flesh of your foreskins, and it shall be a sign of the covenant between me and you. . . . Any uncircumcised male who is not circumcised in the flesh of his foreskin shall be cut off from his people; he has broken my covenant." (Gen. 17:9–14)

That act stood as the central, permanent mark of every male's identification with the covenant of God.

However, after Jesus' ascension and the Holy Spirit's descent on the first Christians at Pentecost, the faith's popularity soon spread beyond the bounds of the circumcised. When the vision-inspired apostle Peter took the good news to a battalion of Roman soldiers in a Roman town, they responded by throwing their arms open to the faith he was proclaiming. They experienced a reprise of Pentecost. What did he do? He baptized these uncircumcised men "in the name of Jesus Christ" (Acts 10:48).

Controversy exploded among the believers. The singular, central mark of being in covenant with God—one that Jesus received as a Jewish infant—was tossed aside by that one act of the leading apostle. The first synodical council meeting was called (Acts 15). All of the disbursed apostles traveled to the city of Jerusalem to take Peter to task—and Paul with him, as he also had been baptizing uncircumcised Gentiles.

The meeting was called to order by James, the brother of Jesus. An intense debate erupted. Some who were associated with the Pharisees and, accordingly, intent on maintaining biblical standards spoke up for the clear, absolute requirement for all male covenanters to be circumcised. Others, especially Peter and Paul, argued that we shouldn't put such an impediment in the way of would-be converts.

James read the final verdict: circumcision was no longer required. How can that be? Who authorized them to dismiss a clear and unequivocal biblical standard? They failed even to cite a single quote from Jesus as validation! Well, they did cite a few biblical standards to hold on to: not eating food polluted by idols, nor strangled meat, nor blood, and avoiding fornication (Acts. 15:29). But those four rules sure looked like a dumbing down of the Ten Commandments and of the other six-hundred-plus biblical commandments the rabbis of the time cited as binding on the children of the covenant.

What's worse, it wouldn't be long before the apostle Paul would soften the rule about associating with idolatrous practices (see 1 Cor. 8:1–13; 10:1–32):

> If an unbeliever invites you to a meal and you are disposed to go, eat whatever is set before you without raising any questions on the ground of conscience. But if someone says to you, "This has been offered in sacrifice," then do not eat it, out of consideration for the one who informed you, and for the sake of conscience—I mean for the others' own. (10:27–29)

In other words, it doesn't matter if the meat served to you has been used in the worship of idols; it won't harm you. Only refrain from eating it if your pagan host says it was so used—given that such an admission shows that that person is feeling guilty.

In other words, "Don't ask; don't tell."

Softening of the Categories

So how did they conclude as they did? How did they dare look at the laws of the Torah, even the requirement for initiation into the covenant, as something less than absolute?

We need to take an honest look at the whole Bible and humbly search for an integrative interpretive framework. We need to excavate the interpretive framework used by Jesus and his apostles—one that acknowledges that the Bible is, indeed, God's word while still including the ambiguities, contradictions, paradoxes, ironies, and mysteries found in it. What we need is a truly Christian ethic, an integrative Christian ethic that reads the Bible on its own terms.

An integrative Christian ethic has to take seriously the commands taught in the Bible. Then again, it must take seriously the episodes in the Bible that fly in the face of the commands taught in the Bible. Further, it must take seriously the ways some commands get countered or qualified by other commands. It also must take seriously the ways Jesus and the apostles revamp some texts from the Hebrew Bible, or the Old Testament. In other words, it must treat the Bible's ambiguities as seriously as it treats the Bible's points of emphasis and consistency.

Ultimately, an integrative ethic requires us to take seriously the fact that God has been revealed to us most centrally as a living Savior. That is, God has chosen to give us not a rule book nor a constitution and bylaws but a person.

A Complicated Savior

As an eighteen-year-old, first-semester freshman in a conservative Pentecostal Bible college, I chose for my first term paper the topic "The Emotions of Jesus as Depicted in the Gospel of Mark." As the son of a psychology professor, I thought the topic could yield some interesting insights. For my research I did the obvious: I read through Mark, circling every word, phrase, or verse that exhibited some expression of emotion by the Savior.

I nearly lost my faith. The Jesus I found in the Gospel of Mark was so incredibly human, demonstrating such a range of feelings, tones of voice, postures toward others, and judgments that it shook me to my toes. What's more, just a week before starting that semester I had viewed the hit movie *Jesus Christ Superstar*, in which Jesus was portrayed as a rather namby-pamby, weak-kneed, pathetic figure (in contrast to Judas Iscariot, who came across as a man of courage and conviction).

With the movie's images in my mind's eye and Mark's language about Jesus in my mind's categories, my faith was discombobulated. In Pentecostal fashion, I asked my three roommates to lay on healing hands and pray for me as I was typing the final draft. I feared that I was losing my faith. Fortunately that fear did not materialize. My faith rebounded. But by then that paper had introduced me to a different Jesus than I'd heard of in Sunday school. Jesus no longer floated on air. He became for me one whose life and teachings were—and remain—seriously contoured, widely nuanced, and broadly ranged.

Of course, on this point, I was just a slow learner. Two millennia ago, the Holy Spirit needed to inspire not just one or two but four writers—four news bureaus—to tell Jesus' life story. And the Spirit inspired several other writers to tell more about Jesus' story, which they explained via personal letters, public epistles, and visionary images (i.e., the book of Revelation)—so that later generations could possess sufficient knowledge of him on which to base their lives.

An integrative Christian ethic needs to be seriously contoured, widely nuanced, and broadly ranged as well. The God who inspired the writing of the Holy Scriptures did so by using many writers and characters just as nuanced and complicated as Jesus himself.

Primary Principles for Living

No, the category "absolutes" does not apply per se to human behavioral requirements. So are we now left in the dark? Certainly not. On several occasions Jesus was asked if there is any commandment that rises above the rest, one that is the greatest of all. He answered, yes, there is: the one, or rather, the two rules about love.

Shall we thus call love an absolute? Well, not really—if only because love is often confused with enabling, indulging, and illicit actions. Perhaps we can call love an overarching, summarizing, guiding principle— for living. In fact, there are two love principles: love of God and love of neighbor.

Jesus spelled out these two primary principles: "'You shall love the Lord your God with all your heart, and with all your soul, and with all your mind.' This is the greatest and first commandment. And a second is like it: 'You shall love your neighbor as yourself.'" (Matt. 22:37–39). In Matthew's Gospel, Jesus adds, "'On these two commandments hang all the law and the prophets'" (v. 40).

Mark's version differs slightly from Matthew's. When asked by a Pharisee-lawyer which commandment in the law is the greatest, "Jesus answered, 'The first is, "Hear, O Israel: the Lord our God, the Lord is one; you shall love the Lord your God with all your heart, and with all your soul, and with all your mind, and with all your strength." The second is this, "You shall love your neighbor as yourself."'" Mark then adds Jesus' rejoinder: "'There is no other commandment greater than these'" (Mark 12:29–31).

In Luke's account, it is a lawyer who gives the answer: "Just then a lawyer stood up to test Jesus. 'Teacher,' he said, 'what must I do to inherit eternal life?' He said to him, 'What is written in the law? What do you read there?' He answered, 'You shall love the Lord your God with all your heart, and with all your soul, and with all your strength, and with all your mind; and your neighbor as yourself.' And he said to him, 'You have given the right answer; do this, and you will live'" (Luke 10:25–28).

So, while each of the Synoptic Gospel writers presents a different nuance—Jesus' central command was likely repeated many times and in many ways over his three-year public ministry—the point is clear: to love God with all that is in you and to love neighbor as yourself stand as the primary guiding principles for living. They summarize all of the commandments of God.

By stating without hesitation that these two commandments are "the first of all," Jesus is also implying that other commandments are not. By implication then, not all commandments were created equal. Jesus is stating clearly that, at least to some degree, the commandments carry different levels of rank status.

That does not mean that other commandments don't count. Rather it means that these two provide a summary of the rest. They amplify and provide interpretive intentions to the other laws. They define the spirit of the particular laws. And from them derive all of the other commandments of God.

More Than a Guiding Principle

The specific derivations and delineations of particular laws still remain important. While all of the laws and writings of the Prophets do depend on the commandments to love God and neighbor, the specific components of loving specified in various places and in various ways in Scripture give specificity to the general principles of living.

Rightly so. It is not enough simply to idealize or sentimentalize the command to love. In fact, Christian love is not merely a sweet sentiment. It is an action, a costly giving of oneself to God in service to God as well as to other people. It is carried out in specific ways that are visible, tangible, and measureable—requiring specific actions in order to effect specific ends.

Those derivations of the primary principles for living fall into several categories. We will look in some detail at the first, which I call aspirations, in the remainder of this chapter. We will then explore three additional categories in chapter 4—1) standards or benchmarks, 2) applications, and 3) approximations and adaptations.

Aspirations

Aspirations? In medical terms, one aspires a breath and/or bodily fluids. In public speaking terms, aspiration has to do with making one's breath audible. But in terms of ethics and behavior, to aspire is to yearn—to seek to achieve something great, noble, or excellent. And the term also refers to the object of such a desire.

Often biblical writers and speakers urge others to aspire to something higher than themselves or, at least, higher than their base instincts. "'But strive [or seek] first for the kingdom of God and his righteousness, and all these things will be given to you as well,'" said Jesus (Matt. 6:33). Jesus does not imply that the kingdom of God would be fully realized by the seeker, but he certainly was suggesting that one could and should invest oneself to pursue such a realization. I am reminded of the immortal words of former

President Theodore Roosevelt delivered in a speech in Paris, France, in 1910:

> It is not the critic who counts; not the man who points out how the strong man stumbles, or where the doer of deeds could have done them better. The credit belongs to the man who is actually in the arena, whose face is marred by dust and sweat and blood; who strives valiantly; who errs, who comes short again and again, because there is no effort without error and shortcoming; but who does actually strive to do the deeds; who knows great enthusiasms, the great devotions; who spends himself in a worthy cause; who at the best knows in the end the triumph of high achievement, and who at the worst, if he fails, at least fails while daring greatly, so that his place shall never be with those cold and timid souls who neither know victory nor defeat."[1]

So it is with aspirations. If carefully chosen, they draw us upward and outward. They elevate us above our more crass and self-serving instincts. They deepen our feelings. They broaden our vision. They empower our resolve. They help overcome impediments and correct misdirections. For aspirations to do those things requires not only that we apply ourselves but also that we choose our aspirations well. So what aspirations should believers adopt as their own?

Let me suggest seven ways to love God and then seven ways to love our neighbors. The number seven is chosen not because it is magical or, as it is often claimed to be, the number of perfection. Rather, a thorough study of both the Scriptures and the historic confessions of the faith has revealed fourteen different ways to love— half of them toward God and half toward others.

Loving God: Seven Aspirations

The following seven aspirations are specific ways a believer can seek to pursue the command to love God with all of one's heart, soul, strength, and mind:

1. Theodore Roosevelt, "Citizenship in a Republic" (speech, Sorbonne, Paris, France, April 23, 1910).

1. Glorify God. "What is the chief end of man [sic]? Man's chief end is to glorify God and to enjoy him forever."[2] This question and answer launch the Smaller Catechism of the Westminster Confession. Through the past four centuries it may well be the most quoted expression of the Christian faith outside of the Bible itself, and for good reason. It summarizes a theme that runs throughout the Scriptures:

> The heavens are telling the glory of God;
>> and the firmament proclaims his handiwork.
>>> (Ps. 19:1)

> And suddenly there was with the angel a multitude of the heavenly host, praising God and saying,
>> "Glory to God in the highest heaven,
>>> and on earth peace among those whom he favors!"
>>>> (Luke 2:13–14)

> "In the same way, let your light shine before others, so that they may see your good works and give glory to your Father in heaven."
>> (Matt. 5:16)

> For you were bought with a price; therefore glorify God in your body.
>> (1 Cor. 6:20)

> So, whether you eat or drink, or whatever you do, do everything for the glory of God.
>> (1 Cor. 10:31)

The Bible's call to glorify God arises in many contexts and comes in many forms. What does it mean, in essence? Well, historically it has found primary focus in the act of worship, and rightly so as pictured especially in the exalted expressions of praise presented in the

---

2. *The Constitution of the Presbyterian Church (U.S.A.)*, Part I, *Book of Confessions* (Louisville, KY: Office of the General Assembly, Presbyterian Church (U.S.A.), 1999), 7.001.

prophets' visions of God—such as those of Isaiah and Ezekiel—and in John's apocalyptic visions in the book of Revelation.

But does human worship provide God anything more than an ego boost, like the feeling felt when a crowd applauds your piano recital or your gymnastics routine? Well, think of the framed canvas expressing the beauty in an artist's imagination. Think of an orchestra performing the sounds heard in the inner ear of a composer. Think of a custom-built home being a monument to the vision of the architect. God the Creator is the artist, composer, and architect of a universe intended to express the beauty, harmony, and composition inherent in God's own character.

Accordingly, humans glorify God in any acts of service and piety outside church buildings. As Paul tells the Roman Christians, "I appeal to you therefore, brothers and sisters, by the mercies of God, to present your bodies as a living sacrifice, holy and acceptable to God, which is your spiritual worship" (Rom. 12:1). Any act of consecration, service, sharing, or affection gives tangible expression of God's character in the world and thus qualifies as worship. To glorify God is to let the light of God's character be reflected back for God to enjoy. To aspire to do so is to express the highest form of loving God.

2. **Fear/revere God.** The writer of Proverbs defines the book's thesis in the prologue: "The fear of the LORD is the beginning of knowledge" (1:7). Similarly, Isaiah's vision of God caused him to cower in awe-filled fear:

> In the year that King Uzziah died, I saw the Lord sitting on a throne, high and lofty; and the hem of his robe filled the temple. Seraphs were in attendance above him; each had six wings: with two they covered their faces, and with two they covered their feet, and with two they flew. And one called to another and said:
>
> "Holy, holy, holy is the LORD of hosts;
> the whole earth is full of his glory."
>
> The pivots on the thresholds shook at the voices of those who called, and the house filled with smoke. And I said: "Woe is me! I am lost, for I am a man of unclean lips, and I live among a people of unclean lips; yet my eyes have seen the King, the LORD of hosts!" (Isa. 6:1–5)

To treat God as God means that we approach God with awe and reverence. We fear the possibility of taking God for granted. We shun the tendency of using God's name as a tool for our own use. We resist the temptation to simplify God (a central reason why the creating of images of God is prohibited in the Second Commandment). Instead, we aspire to honor God as God is.

3. Adore God. The flip side of fear is adoration. Fear puts us at God's feet. Adoration draws us to God's breast. Like the infant in its mother's arms, the child of God is invited to feel the tenderness of God's consuming love.

While the use of the names Father and Son have generated resistance in this era of gender inclusion—and understandably so—it's important that we don't miss the major point of Jesus' use of such labeling. God is named as Father eight times in the Hebrew Scriptures whereas that name appears on Jesus' lips over two hundred times in the Gospels. Why such a point of emphasis? Well, it wasn't to stress God's gender. It was to express tenderness. The God to whom Jesus was reintroducing his people is a God who loves like the shepherd who leaves behind the ninety-nine sheep to find the one that is missing. It is a God who loves like a mother hen who draws her chicks under her wing or like a father who runs to the crest of the hill to welcome home his prodigal son. To adore God is to receive that tender love and to reciprocate.

4. Trust God. Time and again the Scriptures call persons to believe in God. To place your faith in God implies more than verbal assent. It means to entrust your life into the hands of God. It means to give yourself to God's service and to count on God to oversee, to guide providentially, and to lead to pastures green. Jesus adds, " 'Do not let your hearts be troubled. Believe in God, believe also in me'" (John 14:1).

5. Take up your cross and follow Christ. When calling the original twelve disciples, Jesus repeatedly made the appeal for them to take up their own crosses and follow him. The language certainly escaped their comprehension at the time, for none imagined the crucifixion that awaited their leader. Surely none imagined the prospect of a martyrdom that might bring their own end.

Still, the language does underline a level of total commitment between the disciples and Jesus to which he challenged them and all other followers. Their resulting willingness to pay the ultimate price—carrying one's cross—takes this commitment to the highest level.

6. Put on the mind of Christ. Pressing still further into loving God—especially with one's mind—calls for thinking differently. Given that God calls us "to be conformed to the image of" Christ (Rom. 8:29), one key path toward that goal is to imbibe the mind of Christ: to think as Jesus thought, to develop the kind of God-centeredness, eternal perspective, and rightly prioritized mind-set that was exemplified by Jesus in his incarnation.

In that light, the apostle Paul exhorted the Romans, "Do not be conformed to this world, but be transformed by the renewing of your minds, so that you may discern what is the will of God—what is good and acceptable and perfect" (Rom. 12:2). He also assured the Corinthians that that transformation really can happen: "'For who has known the mind of the Lord so as to instruct him?' But we have the mind of Christ" (1 Cor. 2:16).

7. Keep the Lord's Day holy. This aspiration jars most twenty-first-century Americans. In a culture that knows few "blue laws," Sunday buzzes with the same energy as do Monday and Tuesday, studies with the same intensity as Wednesday and Thursday, and plays with the same verve as Friday and Saturday.

But that lack of distinctiveness marks only the Sundays of the past fifty years. Prior to the 1960s, virtually all monotheists set aside one day of the week for rest and spiritual renewal. The only argument was which day should be set aside: "Saturdays," said Jews and Seventh-day Adventists; "Fridays," said Muslims; "Sundays," said most Christians. The gradual secularization of Christendom America since World War II unleashed the profit motives and playful instincts once held in check on Sabbath days, and, as they say, the rest is history.

Still, children of the covenant in virtually all times and places since Moses' day have hallowed one day of the week. They have curbed their own desires and ambitions to conform to that nonnegotiable standard. And as persons of earnest faith, they have invested their hearts into the worship of God on those days.

Christians, in particular, have hallowed Sundays as the Lord's Day, so named since it is the day on which the Lord Jesus rose from the dead. And consistent with the letter to the Hebrews, the day of rest comes not as payoff for six days of work (the Hebrew Sabbath) but as the beginning point of a life lived in grace: starting the week with rest in Jesus' mercy and grace and then following with six days of service driven by gratitude for his indescribable gift.

While the particulars may have changed recently, the search for Sabbath rest remains a central process of spiritual growth and faithful worship—an aspiration worth renewing.

Loving Neighbors: Seven Aspirations

How shall we love our neighbors as ourselves? Again, the study of the Scripture and confessions of the faith have revealed seven paths to pursue.

1. **"Do unto others what you would have them do unto you."** This first people-oriented aspiration is a bit wordy compared to the others, but its central function throughout the Judeo-Christian world—indeed within virtually all religions the world over—requires that it be heard on its own terms. Its point is so self-evident that it requires little explanation except, perhaps, the clarification that its focus on the neighbor does not negate the self-love that it acknowledges as a given. Still, its central point is attentiveness to "the other."

2. **Tell the truth.** Spelled out in the Decalogue as "You shall not bear false witness against your neighbor" (Exod. 20:16), this aspiration states the obvious: "Honesty is the best policy." Or as witnesses are asked in a court of law, "Do you solemnly swear to tell the truth, the whole truth and nothing but the truth?" Jesus' promise "'You will know the truth, and the truth will make you free'" (John 8:32) highlights the value of truth telling. It liberates. It also promotes candor and integrity in relationships where secrecy and deceit would damage.

For believers, the task of truth telling also adds a capital T: bearing witness to the eternal Truth of the gospel of Jesus Christ. Accordingly, Jesus' final words prior to his ascension commission his followers: "'But you will receive power when the Holy Spirit has come upon you; and you will be my witnesses in Jerusalem, in all Judea and Samaria, and to the ends of the earth'" (Acts 1:8).

3. **Do justice.** Justice is a subject so large that it requires a chapter all its own, so we will tackle it at length in chapter 6. But for the moment, the centrality of the words of Micah spell out the centrality of this theme in Scripture:

He has told you, O mortal, what is good;
  and what does the LORD require of you
but to do justice, and to love kindness,
  and to walk humbly with your God?

(Mic. 6:8)

4. Be a steward. The economy of God—rising far above those of both capitalism and socialism—is that of stewardship. To be a steward is to treat the valuables in hand as trusts to be managed as the farm manager oversees the sowing and reaping on behalf of the property's owner or the flight attendant oversees the airplane on behalf of the corporation (present-day flight attendants used to be called "stewards" and "stewardesses.")

One of the greatest theological advances of the twentieth century was the blossoming of the biblical study of the environment. The field was birthed especially by Holmes Rolston III, a pastor who shifted into a vocation as professor of the philosophy of science and who read the Bible with one eye and beheld God's creation with the other.

Rolston and others have reminded us that God not only created but also entrusted that creation to humans to manage it. God's creation mandate commands, "'Be fruitful and multiply, and fill the earth and subdue it; and have dominion over the fish of the sea and over the birds of the air and over every living thing that moves upon the earth'"(Gen. 1:28).

Our subsequent care of that creation has been erratic at best, with earlier generations keeping hands off in the Middle Ages and with post-Reformation generations unleashing an industrial revolution that often exploited it. But the renewal of stewardship as a process of faithfully tending God's property is helping us to put it all back into perspective. Ultimately, such a perspective expresses love to folks ranging from next-door neighbors to other-side-of-the-planet folks of future generations.

In all aspects of life—our finances, property, abilities, interpersonal relationships, even our own hopes and dreams—the Christian understands that "our" is a bracketed modifier. We own none of these things. The actual Owner has entrusted them into our care for us to manage, and we will give an accounting in due time for the way in which we have performed our managerial duties.

5. Choose life. "I call heaven and earth to witness against you today that I have set before you life and death, blessings and curses. Choose life so that you and your descendants may live, loving the LORD your God, obeying him, and holding fast to him; for that means life to you and length of days, so that you may live in the land that the LORD swore to give to your ancestors, to Abraham, to Isaac, and to Jacob" (Deut. 30:19–20).

Those words bring to a climactic conclusion the monumental address attributed to Moses as his major farewell address. They actually bracket the whole Torah (Genesis through Deuteronomy) on the creation mandate stated previously. Together, God the creator is empowering humans to be cocreators: persons capable of giving birth to more humans and, indeed, capable of sowing seeds, fertilizing seedlings, and causing life to multiply the world over.

But life brings death—by one means or another. And the possibility of causing an end to life finds its first hints in the end of the mandate: "and subdue it." Accordingly, some of life's most heart-wrenching decisions and bitterest controversies have arisen over these matters. This requires a whole chapter's consideration (chapter 7 to follow).

6. Be faithful. Just the sound of the word *faithful* stirs harmonies and rhythms that sing our best songs. The words "I do promise and covenant before God and these witnesses . . ." evoke images of a bride in her pristine beauty and a groom in his handsomest moment. Thick bridal magazines, pregnant with designer dresses and resort honeymoons, paint pictures in the imaginations of lovers in love.

Right after creating the world, God introduces such partnering with a picture of compatibility and complementarity, disclosure and intimacy, and uniting and childbearing that feels idyllic yet conveys attainability. But then it gets complicated. And while it may have been easy for the first human to recognize which other creature would be a suitable partner—not much competition there—suitability and mutuality have often been an elusive butterfly. Indeed, a controversial moth has often emerged from a caterpillar of hopes and dreams. We will tackle this aspiration in chapter 8.

7. Cultivate community. No one is an island; so goes the familiar cliché. All of us live our lives in the context of community, from the simple pairing of couples to the collection of all humans worldwide.

Throughout recorded history humans have formed relationships of mutual support, and they have organized themselves for the sake of protection, sharing, and nurture.

Faith communities have been organized under directions from God at least since the calling of Abram and Sarai to become parents of the "people of God." Metaphorical terms have accumulated in Scripture to provide multiple angles of insight into its genius and purpose: the "body of Christ," the "family of God," the "temple of the Holy Spirit" among them. Collected together, one cannot but recognize that the church (literally, "called-out ones") has been constituted by God for significant purpose, most especially to show to the world the kind of fellowship—unity in diversity—that marks the very identity of one God in three persons.

Particular to the sweeping themes of this book, faith communities have been formed to share in the practice of discerning God's will in their members' contexts so that God's purposes can be accomplished and that God will be glorified in the process.

From Absolutes to Aspirations

There you have it. In order to love our neighbors as ourselves, we aspire to 1) do unto others what we would have them do unto us, 2) tell the truth, 3) do justice, 4) be stewards, 5) choose life, 6) be faithful, and 7) cultivate community. Combined with the God-loving aspirations to glorify, fear/revere, adore, and trust God as well as to follow and put on the mind of Christ and to keep the Lord's Day holy, they comprise a complete package.

As stated earlier, we will never fully achieve any of these aspirations, but the efforts to do so will draw us closer toward their fulfillment. Indeed, if the vision of their achievement is lofty enough, noble enough, and challenging enough, those aspirations will pull us with a force without which we would achieve little. Their value is well captured in the chapter title "The Relevance of an Impossible Ethical Ideal" in Reinhold Niebuhr's *An Interpretation of Christian Ethics*.[3]

3. Reinhold Niebuhr, *An Interpretation of Christian Ethics*, with a new introduction by Edmund N. Santurri, Library of Theological Ethics (Louisville, KY: Westminster John Knox Press, 2013), 103–35.

Along the way, we will enjoy some of the fruit that such efforts can produce.

Then again, Christian ethics and morals and the discernment of God's will for our lives require us to do more than seek to love. We need to make specific decisions and to take tangible actions in real time. And so did the thousands of persons whose stories were lived out in the collection of stories captured in the biblical record.

How do we take the absolutes about God, the life principles of loving God and neighbor, and the collection of particular aspirations we've outlined and make them work in everyday life? Before we can answer that question fully, we need to look at the remaining three categories that I proposed previously to describe the primary principles of living: 1) benchmarks, or standards, 2) applications, and 3) approximations and adaptations. We will explore each of these in detail in chapter 4.

4

From Aspirations to Adaptations

It's one thing to aspire to do the right thing. It's another thing to do it. In fact, it's another thing to even know what you should try to do in order to do it. Sincere intentions are a good thing, but actions do not always line up with them. People need more guidance than simply their own positive intentions and motives. They need direction. They need roadmaps to follow.

The biblical writers and teachers were not shy about giving specific directions. Readers of the Bible have been quick to quote those teachers that direct them in ways that seem wise, clear, and helpful. But given the irregular and inconsistent ways those particular writers gave particular directives to persons in particular contexts, we who are separated from them by two-to-three thousand years tend to be very selective in our reading of those particular directives.

The specifics within the Ten Commandments have stood the test of time—even if we don't follow them exactly. The 603 additional commands that fill the Torah add more specificity to the Decalogue. But must we follow all of them? If so, how? We have already stated that these commandments do not function as absolutes. Instead we have lifted up the aspirational character of many biblically directional texts as stirring us to pursue honorable and godly, albeit somewhat vague, trajectories. So what are we to make of those other more specific directives?

Answer: treat such biblical teachings as standards or benchmarks; then by observing the ways those standards or benchmarks have become habituated into communal practices, we can dub these practices applications. And then, if we dare be so bold, we will want to take an honest look at how Jesus, his biographers, and subsequent biblical interpreters have reformed such applications in new contexts and situations. This leads us to suggest a new category of approximations and adaptations.

Benchmarks or Standards

When looking for what to do and ways to do it, people instinctively look for guidelines, directives, and/or boundaries to help them get into sync and keep on track. We drive our cars on paved roads, or at least on hard-packed paths, rather than venturing out into open fields. We check speed-limit signs not just to avoid speeding tickets but also to help gauge what kinds of speeds are safe in a particular, especially unfamiliar, environment. Even those who notoriously drive above the speed limit still choose speeds relatively defined by those posted limits.

Benchmarks and/or standards function in a similar way. They give more specific definition to the aspirations that draw us heavenward. They turn lofty concepts into visible, tangible, and measureable tasks and expectations. Indeed they are the yardsticks, the weights and measures, the "industry standards," the best practices against which other things are compared, gauged, and evaluated.

Consider, for example, the aspiration "Glorify God." What does that look like? Well, the most obvious act of God glorification entails worshiping the Lord with the people of God. That is, we gather with other believers to pray, sing, listen, give thanks, and affirm our faith.

Consider the aspiration "Tell the truth." What does that look like? The standard required by the U.S. courts spells it out: "Tell the truth, the whole truth, and nothing but the truth."

We can—and will—spell out general standards or benchmarks for all of the aspirations we outlined in the last chapter. But before doing so, let's define the next on-deck categories of directives: applications and approximations and adaptations.

Applications

So the standard or benchmark for glorifying God is to gather with the people of God to worship the Lord. What does that look like? How does that get applied? Those questions generate a collection of differing responses.

For Roman Catholic, worship is guided by a priest or bishop; it entails carefully ordered rituals, and it culminates in the transubstantiated body of Christ. Pentecostal Christians lift their heads, voices, and hands in expressive, emotional, enthusiastic singing followed by intense and passionate preaching of God's good news. Mainline Protestant and Evangelical Christians tend to find some mix of styles—some leaning toward the liturgy; others focusing on songs, Scripture, and sermon; some sharing in the sacraments of Baptism and Eucharist; others speaking of those acts simply as ordinances; some holding onto ancient, medieval, or "old-time religion" approaches; while others have jettisoned the old in favor of the new.

These characterizations of the world's largest Christian groups beg for analysis of the many other groups whose forms of worship reflect their own convergence of religious heritage, earnest lovers of God who have pursued the ennobling aspiration to glorify God in worship. Ironically, in spite of such a diversity of choices, most branches of the church wax eloquent about the merits of worshiping God in the patterns they have habituated.

Might we all take a step back and acknowledge that each one of these applications of the standard—worshiping the Lord with God's people—can surely bring glory to God? Most of us can nod in humble agreement, even as we stick to the form that most moves us. Still, we are informed and guided in our particular traditions by the ways that our forebears have defined applications of the standards that help us to aspire to glorify God—ultimately aiming to love God with heart, soul, mind, and strength.

Approximations and Adaptations

So the people gather together to worship God—and thereby they are constituted as the church family, the body of Christ, the temple of the Holy Spirit. They hear the Word of God proclaimed; they share in the sacraments (or ordinances); they pray; and they praise.

Except for the members stuck in the hospital. And those in nursing homes. And those away in military service or on business trips. Plus those competing in soccer tournaments and ballet performances and, well, the list goes on. What about their worship of God? Can there possibly be a next-best thing? In the second half of the twentieth century, TV preaching emerged as a backup alternative. While maligned as God-in-a-box by local church pastors, many a believer found such options to be edifying, uplifting, and even a next-best thing. In the twenty-first century, the simplified and economized Internet technologies brought simultaneous or delayed-broadcast worship services into the homes, dorms, and hospital rooms of many a church member.

On the face of it, worshiping at such a distance cannot match the experience of being surrounded by a company of friends and strangers, but shall we fault those who would avail themselves of such options as their backup plan?

Consider the terms *approximate* and *adapt*. While the aspiration to glorify God takes its best form in the standard, benchmark form of corporate worship as applied in the traditions to which each of us subscribes, that standard can be approximated and adapted as circumstances require.

Let's get more specific. To approximate is to measure close to the benchmark. For example, if you stretch out your arms and say, "This is a meter," you are probably incorrect if measuring by exacting standards. But you may well be approximately correct, somewhere around 80 to 120 centimeters, or 35 to 45 inches, unless your arms are exceedingly long or quite short. On the other hand, if you held your right-hand thumb in parallel to your index finger and said, "This is a meter," you most assuredly would be inaccurate, as that space would probably be no more than a few centimeters or a couple of inches.

Going one step further, to adapt is to find a different but equivalent way to accomplish an aspiration. For example, if a Methodist family finds itself far away from home and church on a Sunday and chooses to worship together in ways similar to what their home church is doing, they would be approximating the standard. If, on the other hand, those same family members choose to watch on television the broadcast of a Pentecostal worship service, and they mostly just watch it, we might call that an adaptation.

To suggest the use of such labels as approximation and adaptation—the former being close to the original, the latter being more innovative—is to state the obvious. Throughout the centuries, authentic Christians have lived out their faith by approximating and adapting—often without a second thought.

The Approximated, Adapted Days of Our Lives

Consider the Fourth Commandment, "Remember the sabbath day, and keep it holy" (Exod. 20:8). Above we considered the particular glorifying-God task of worship. But let's press further to the part dealing with work and rest.

While any logical-minded person might consider it arbitrary to set aside one day each week to be holy unto the Lord, the Decalogue did so, and the historic church followed suit until the mid-twentieth century. Indeed, in the 1950s virtually every European and North or South American country—and many others in Asia, Africa, and Australia—protected Sundays, Saturdays, or Friday as holy days unto the Lord.

However, adamant as were pastors and priests about keeping the Lord's Day holy, they themselves never worked as hard as they did on the Lord's Day. Isn't that a bit odd? Granted, their work was being exerted in order to help their parishioners encounter the holy God, but they were still working themselves to the point of exhaustion.

That fact was not lost on the Savior. When the Pharisees indicted him for allowing the disciples to pluck grain, he countered, "'Have you not read in the law that on the sabbath the priests in the temple break the sabbath and yet are guiltless?'" (Matt. 12:5). What did the religious leaders then do? Indeed, what do religious leaders now do with the Sabbath requirements? "I take my Sabbath on Mondays," or Fridays, or some other day, they all say. We follow the Sabbath principle by adaptation: we rest on another day of the week.

In fact, the apostle Paul takes the point to another level. "Some judge one day to be better than another, while others judge all days to be alike. Let all be fully convinced in their own minds. Those who observe the day, observe it in honor of the Lord" (Rom. 14:5–6a). For the Apostle, the key is to honor the Lord. The specific tactics are much less important than the aspiration.

Telling the Truth, Mostly

We can see how a similar sequence unfolds as we seek to tell the truth. As stated, the benchmark/standard is to "tell the truth, the whole truth, and nothing but the truth." However, truth telling can go awry. Truths blurted by one are heard by another as rationalizations, as propagandizing, as "spinning" the truth.

Then again, truths often get spewed like bullets from machine guns. And some blurted truths actually are not true—not because the person isn't being honest but because the person isn't well informed. Inaccuracies are untruths, no matter how sincerely held. The simple act of telling the truth gets confused. Into that standard, the letter to the Ephesians advises that "speaking the truth in love we must grow up in every way into him who is the head, into Christ" (4:15). In other words, the aspiration to tell the truth has to be wedded to the guiding principle of "loving our neighbors as ourselves."

Further, the Bible itself applies the task of truth telling to the particular task of giving witness. In its most essential form it comes as the Ninth Commandment: "You shall not bear false witness" (Exod. 20:16). In Jesus' preascension commission to his disciples, he directs them to become "my witnesses in Jerusalem, in all Judea and Samaria, and to the ends of the earth" (Acts 1:8). Accordingly, the task of telling the truth requires not only the accurate presentation of facts but also the capital-T Truth about Jesus and his work of redemption and reconciliation.

Thus, truth telling requires us to give witness to "what we have seen and heard" (Acts 4:20), whether we find ourselves testifying in a court of law or in a tent revival meeting or whether we are speaking in a stadium or in a private confessional. But its application takes some courage, some finesse, some grace.

Still, there are times when truth telling is simply the wrong thing to do. The most frequent case comes when a child—your daughter, your niece, your granddaughter—asks, "Do you like my new dress?" and you think it looks hideous. Should you report the facts regarding your opinion about the dress, or should you redirect? "You look beautiful in that dress" can be true—because she is beautiful no matter what she is wearing—although that response is not "nothing but the truth." If she presses further, asking, "But do you love this dress?" then the best answer is probably to tell a lie.

Of course, the term "white lie" comes to mind. It is usually a better response than the ugly truth that you simply think that the dress looks hideous, because by saying that you are unnecessarily damaging her self-esteem. Such an adaptation of the aspiration to tell the truth takes on even greater import when ethnic-cleansing militia members knock on the door in search of their intended prey. Honesty is not always the best policy. By the way, Jesus said as much, in the parable of the Dishonest Manager (Luke 16:1–9) cited previously.

Does that mean that truth telling is so hopelessly thrown overboard that nothing remains of it? Certainly not. The benchmark "Bear no false witness" remains the standard. And speaking the truth in love and giving witness to the truth about Jesus stand as apt applications of that standard. But in some cases and in some situations, approximating and adapting the standard can be a fitting way to live forth a Christian ethic and witness.

From Sabbath Keeping and Truth Telling to What?

When we consider these two examples, Sabbath keeping and truth telling, in the light of the actions taken by the Jerusalem Council regarding the eating of food offered to idols, we begin to see a pattern emerging. When we articulate the aspirations by which we best love God and neighbors; benchmark those aspirations in visible, tangible, and measureable ways; and detail these benchmarks/standards as in-context applications, we still find times and circumstances that suggest and perhaps even require us to do otherwise. We find that present context and circumstances may require us to find approximations or even adaptations of a benchmark/standard.

Such approximations and/or adaptations do not negate the corresponding aspirations, benchmarks/standards, or applications. Those ideas and scales of measuring remain in place even while those approximations and/or adaptations test the boundaries of such possibilities. Let's now consider other ways that we regularly approximate and adapt our aspirations and benchmarks.

Trusting God

Take, for example, the aspiration to trust God. One need not read much of the New Testament to notice that such trust is highly rated. From the references to Abraham's having "'believed God, and it was reckoned to him as righteousness'" (Gal. 3:6), to John's having written his whole Gospel so that readers "may come to believe that Jesus is the Messiah, the Son of God, and that through believing . . . have life in his name" (20:31), Christ followers are compelled to believe in God, that is, to trust in Jesus. That's the primary gateway into a life of spiritual abundance.

So how does one benchmark such an aspiration? One does so by jettisoning all doubts about God's existence, identity, good intentions, and faithfulness. When asked, "'How did the fig tree wither at once?'" Jesus responded,

> "Truly I tell you, if you have faith and do not doubt, not only will you do what has been done to the fig tree [cause it to wither], but even if you say to this mountain, 'Be lifted up and thrown into the sea,' and it will be done. Whatever you ask for in prayer with faith, you will receive." (Matt. 21:21–22)

Then again, do believers ever believe so totally that no hint of doubt remains in their thinking? "I believe; help my unbelief!" (Mark 9:24), uttered the father of a spirit-possessed son to Jesus, and the Savior liberated the boy from his suffering.

But let's press the point further. If we are to trust God in all things, should we jettison gainful employment in order to serve as mission workers and just trust God to provide all our needs? The mendicants, or beggar monks, who formed an order in 1210 CE count St. Francis of Assisi and St. Domenic as their founders. Their model of raising funds through panhandling allows them to uphold a prohibition against owning any property either as individuals or in common. But when Christians in first-century Thessalonica did that, Paul excoriated them:

> Now we command you, beloved, in the name of our Lord Jesus Christ, to keep away from believers who are living in

idleness and not according to the tradition that they received from us. For you yourselves know how you ought to imitate us; we were not idle when we were with you, and we did not eat anyone's bread without paying for it; but with toil and labor we worked night and day, so that we might not burden any of you. . . . Anyone unwilling to work should not eat. (2 Thess. 3:6–8, 10)

Pressing the point further still, is it unfaithful to save money for a rainy day or to invest for retirement or even to purchase life insurance? Is it wrong to plan for the future? Well, when addressing building efforts or military campaigns, Jesus suggested the need for calculated planning:

For which of you, intending to build a tower, does not first sit down and estimate the cost, to see whether he has enough to complete it? Otherwise, when he has laid a foundation and is not able to finish, all who see it will begin to ridicule him, saying, "This fellow began to build and was not able to finish." (Luke 14:28–32)

Yes, all believers need to put their trust in God, specifically entrusting their lives into God's hand. But they also need to work—usually for gainful remuneration—and they need to plan for future needs, including retirement.

Does it sound odd to think that the same Scriptures that lift up such ideas as "trust in the Lord with all your heart" also adapt such idealism in such pragmatic ways? Most believers find it completely natural to blend such idealisms with practicalities. Approximating and adapting is the norm, not an exception or an oddity.

Adoring God

Consider the aspiration to adore God. Given that we are to love God with all of our heart, soul, mind, and strength, our affections need to be warmed toward God. Toward that end, earnest believers will seek to develop such spiritual disciplines as personal prayer and meditation in communion with God. How shall we benchmark such actions?

Paul provides a clear benchmark: "Pray without ceasing" (1 Thess. 5:17). That's right: unceasing prayer—which by implication generates uninterrupted communing and abiding with God. Who could fault you for that? Then again, which of us would like to live with somebody praying unceasingly? The phrase "So heavenly minded that they're no earthly good" comes to mind.

Accordingly, through the ages churches have typically recommended the development of a cluster of spiritual disciplines that include a relatively brief session of prayer in the morning and evening or perhaps a series of prayer times, such as are observed in Muslim communities. And they have enhanced that by organizing prayer meetings to cultivate prayer partnerships. In either case, the benchmark of "pray without ceasing" gets applied via regular spiritual discipline and then approximated and adapted by the commonly erratic and irregular process for forming such habits in a world of unrelenting interruptions.

Taking Up Your Cross to Follow Jesus

So how do you benchmark taking up your cross? How do we measure following Jesus? Perhaps the best way is to develop a rhythm of repenting our sins, receiving Christ's forgiveness, and presenting our bodies as a living sacrifice to God (Rom. 12:1). In so doing we can resolve to reform our ways to be more obedient to God's will and more earnest in our Christian service. While spiritual growth is difficult to measure, the exercise of such spiritual disciplines assures that one is taking the right steps to be a more faithful follower of Jesus.

This benchmark has been applied corporately in churches' exercise of discipline. Many branches of the church ask newly joining members to commit themselves to a life of discipleship by submitting themselves to the discipline of the church. Indeed, the churches of the Scottish Reformation speak of the "notes of the church" as being not just the Word rightly proclaimed and the sacraments rightly administered but also discipline righty exercised.

Such discipline most often gets exercised in informal ways, as when one believer "speaks the truth in love" (Eph. 4:15) with another believer. Still, it can move into formalized and even judicial practices, aiming to restore those who have erred and to inspire all others to aim to follow God's will.

Putting on the Mind of Christ

What better way to follow Jesus effectively and to become more and more conformed to his image (Rom. 8:29) than to learn to think as he thought? Benchmarking this transformation of the mind (Rom. 12:2) naturally entails developing regular habits of Bible reading, ideally as a daily discipline; of theological study; and of dialoguing with others about the faith, most fittingly in a regularly scheduled learning fellowship such as a church-school class or a home Bible-study group.

Accordingly, churches have applied and regularized such study habits by following the ancient practice of daily lectionary readings, engaging in the Sunday school movement (a nineteenth-century invention), participating in the home-group study practices introduced by the early Methodists and made popular in youth and college fellowships, and participating in the home-study practices that arose in the twentieth century. Through the ages, however, great Christian leaders have also applied themselves in other academic disciplines, developing expertise in all of the arts and sciences—from the heights of philosophy to the depths of psychology, from the particularities of molecular biology to the mysteries of black holes. Followers of Christ have also turned their talents into profound expressions of their faith; such names as Bach and Handel, Michelangelo and Rembrandt come to mind.

Can we cite chapter and verse in the Bible to press this point? Paul's quotation of a Greek poet and his naming of the unknown God in Athens (Acts 17:22–31) show how he was both informed by and made use of his cultural literacy to serve God's high purposes for his life. So, too, all of us, while aiming to put on the mind of Christ and seeking to be transformed by the renewing of our minds, do well to carefully explore our major field of study, the Scriptures, and to adapt our study efforts by developing acuity in a broad range of learning.

Doing unto Others as You Would
Have Them Do unto You

While making room for approximations and adaptions in the pursuit of these God-ward aspirations, we need to apply such reasoning in our neighborly directions. The most obvious way to follow the love commandment is to follow the Golden Rule. This ethic of reciprocity is found in most all of the major religions. It does not originate with Jesus, although he certainly gave it great prominence.

So how can one turn that maxim into a benchmark? One can do so simply by elevating its character values of equality, generosity, and servanthood. Churches have applied the Golden Rule by setting up missional outreach programs. They range from feeding the poor and clothing the naked to proclaiming the gospel and translating Scripture into hundreds of languages.

But should we always do this? Again human experience has taught us that the aspiration, noble as it sounds, can backfire. Twelve-step programs warn friends and family members not to become enablers of the addicts they love. Too often others, spouses especially, actually reinforce their partners' addictive tendencies by being too generous, too accommodating, and too supportive. Tough love, blunt confrontations, and disregard sometimes better serve the person in trouble. Yes, the motive—to do unto others—remains, but it needs to be approximated and adapted sometimes by doing the opposite of what one's intuition and generous inclinations would dictate.

Being a Steward

So how shall we benchmark the mind-set of stewardship? As any minister can attest, any member whose framework shifts from that of an independent owner to that of an interdependent steward undergoes a tectonic shift. Most stewards testify that the shift took place when they instituted the practice of tithing: keeping 90 percent of all of their commodities while presenting one-tenth (the meaning of *tithe*) of their property, earnings, and/or time to the Lord through the local church. Soon, they discover the joy of giving to other causes, charities, and mission work. "They even become the most generous tippers in restaurants," says Karl Travis, a pastor and popular conference speaker on the subject.

Might approximations and adaptations play a part in all of this? Of course! For those who are deeply indebted, facing financial setback after setback and having to choose between feeding their children and tithing, there is plenty of room for smaller percentages to be given. Tithing—giving 10 percent—sets a benchmark. It does not serve as a definitive command.

Classical Schools of Thought

The core reasoning that drives the formulation of integrative Christian ethics is that this model reflects the rationale behind so many passages of Scripture. It simply fits holy writ. However, a reinforcing line of reasoning for such thinking arises from the integration of the two chief approaches used in classical philosophical ethics.

All the way back to ancient Greece and beyond, teleological ethics has tended to dominate the field. Drawn from the Greek word *telos*, which means finish line, the good is defined as what brings the best result, the greatest good, to the greatest number of people. The love ethic, in particular the Golden Rule, stands at the center of this ethic. Its greatest proponent was none other than Aristotle himself.

Then again, also drawing from the ancients is the school of deontological ethics. It places its focus on the role of the law in shaping and corralling human behavior. Its greatest proponent and expositor is Immanuel Kant, although the name of a far more ancient person, Moses, also comes to mind. What's right, says the deontologist, is what the laws say is right. Of course the formulation of laws is somewhat fluid, but common-sense laws fit into those propounded in legislatures. And ultimately, the consensus of a society generally and eventually does prevail, and one should follow such prescriptions.

In the second half of the twentieth century, Joseph Fletcher pushed ethical and moral reasoning into the national conversation with the publication of his widely read *Situation Ethics: The New*

Morality.[1] New? Tell that to Aristotle. Fletcher largely was popularizing Aristotelian teleology. In the process, his single-minded advocacy for the loving thing and dismissive rejection of any other kind of law exposed the hollowness of teleological ethics when taken to their logical conclusion. On the other hand, anyone familiar with Jesus' arguments with the Pharisees and scribes knows how he repeatedly exposed the hollowness of their loveless obsession with law enforcement. The legalisms they promoted, which were echoed within the church years later, especially in Galatia, stole grace from the gospel. So many proponents of either of these schools have addressed the masses like a table server who says, "Here is the salt, and here is the pepper. You can use either one, but you cannot use both."

My proposal for a new, integrative Christian ethic is one that says with normal table servers, "Enjoy the salt and pepper together!" To be exact, this ethical formulation begins teleologically: Love God and neighbor. It waxes deontological by casting a vision for fourteen aspirations and then benchmarking them as standards. It reports on the ways those standards are regularly applied. But then it leans back in the teleological direction, asking how the law can be approximated and adapted for the particular context at the time.

Moving from the reductionism of a monovalent option for either the rule of law or the rule of love to the multivalent option to be informed and guided by both the rule of law and the rule of love not only better reflects the aggregate teachings of the Scriptures but also works in real life. It is how honest and authentic Christians are discerning God's will every day—whether they know it or not. Hence, the two schools of thought join hands in partnership to truly help persons of good will discern God's will in their lives and in their world.

So What's This All Look Like?

Jesus and the apostles did not have a spreadsheet with which to systematize the ethical and moral teachings they were promoting. But

1. Joseph Fletcher, *Situation Ethics: The New Morality* (Louisville, KY: Westminster John Knox Press, 1997).

with the benefits of modern technology I would visualize what we have said so far in the ways shown in tables 1 and 2.

Some categories remain blank at the moment. We will fill in those blanks over the course of the next three chapters.

Table 1: Love God with Heart, Soul, Mind, and Strength

Aspirations	Standards / Benchmarks	Applications	Approximations and Adaptations
Glorify God.	Worship the Lord with people of God.	Participate in weekly church worship, with Word and Sacraments.	Worship via TV or Internet.
Fear/revere God.			
Adore God.	Pray without ceasing; commune with God constantly.	Exercise daily discipline of individual prayer and weekly practice of group prayer.	Don't be so spiritually minded that you are no earthly good.
Trust God.	Believe in Jesus; entrust your whole life into his hands; and do not doubt.	In gratitude, demonstrate your faith via devotion and service.	Invest; plan for a rainy day, for retirement, etc.
Take up your cross and follow Christ.	Confess; forgive; and obey.	Submit to church accountability and discipline.	Incorporate ambition, initiative, and industry.
Put on the mind of Christ.	Be transformed; renew your mind; study the Word.	Participate in daily personal and weekly group Bible study; learn from multiple sources.	Study broadly; be informed from multiple sources.
Keep the Lord's Day holy.	Keep the Lord's Day holy, setting it aside for worship and spiritual renewal.	Don't work on the Lord's Day; enjoy rest, relaxation, and the rekindling of relationships.	Use the alternative rhythm of rest/renewal if working on Sundays (e.g., ministers).

Table 2: Love Your Neighbor as Yourself

Aspirations	Standards / Benchmarks	Applications	Approximations and Adaptations
"Do unto others what you would have them do unto you."	Be generous; serve strangers and enemies, widows and orphans.	Engage in and support missional outreaches and charitable causes.	Resist deception and addiction-enabling; set priorities for constructive giving.
Tell the truth.	Tell the truth, the whole truth, and nothing but the truth.	Report the facts; give witness to the Truth (Jesus), and speak the truth in love.	Tell white lies for kindness' sake; exercise respectful caution when giving a witness.
Do justice.			
Be a steward.	Treat all assets as God's property.	Tithe time, talents, and treasure; recycle; care for the creation.	Consume resources as needed for good; enjoy the 90 percent.
Choose life.			
Be faithful.			
Cultivate community: people of God, body of Christ, temple of the Spirit.			

Altogether Now

It is quite a move to start at the guiding principles of love for God and love for neighbor and then to articulate fourteen aspirations that both specify and facilitate the fulfillment of those guiding principles. It's an even bigger move to take those fourteen aspirations and articulate corresponding benchmark/standards for each—as well as applications most often put into action. Then, with the addition of corresponding approximations and adaptations, you may feel like you're suffering from intellectual backlash.

However, most of the claims made in this chapter and most of the movements from guiding principles to approximations and adaptations are ones you readily recognize in your own way of assessing what to do at any given time. Let's now move ahead to take a closer look at those aspirations that will require more time to unpack.

5

How to Be Both Countercultural and Contextually Relevant without Frying Your Smartphone

Together we have been talking about ways particular aspirations lead to the formulation of standards/ benchmarks, which then find specificity in applications while still leaving room for approximations and adaptations. I trust you have noticed that they've mostly been pretty obvious. Once you read through the first few, you probably anticipated what was coming in those that followed, but you also noticed that some of the aspirations were skipped. That's because a few beg for deeper treatment. They are so enormous, complex, and/or contested that we will want to discuss them in greater detail. In this chapter I want to discuss two of them.

The first topic shines the light on assumptions underlying most values convictions. Like the proverbial elephant in the living room or the waters in which the fish swim, it is so big and ubiquitous that it seldom gets noticed and almost never gets named. Yet all of our actions and all of our convictions reflect our assumptions (too often ill-considered) about it. The second topic is summarized by a word that generates passion in some of us and a dismissive shrug in others. The Bible gives top billing to both of these topics: 1) "Fearing God," and 2) "Doing Justice."

Fearing and Revering

At first glance, the very thought of fearing God brings a knee-jerk response among Christians. "That's the God of the Old Testament," blurt many—especially those who are forgetting the story of the demise of Ananias and Sapphira in Acts 5 or the ban placed on particular sinners in 1 Corinthians 5 and 2 Thessalonians 3. In fact, the God who creates the universe in Genesis 1 is the same one enthroned in Revelation 22; the God who condemns idolatry at Mt. Sinai is the same one commending Moses on the Mount of Transfiguration.

But "perfect love casts out all fear" respond many others (correctly citing 1 John 4:18). Yet if that were literally true in all cases and at all times, how could the author of those six confident words also write the book of Revelation, in which the works of God incite fear? To be sure, the apostle John's exalted vision of love casting out fear does not erase the other biblical citations that commend or even command it.

How can the negative emotion of fear be "the beginning of wisdom" (Prov. 9:10)? Well, to posture oneself before God in a state of fear—a word also translated "awe" and "reverence"—is to see God as Isaiah did (as previously cited):

> In the year that King Uzziah died, I saw the Lord. . . . And I said: "Woe is me! I am lost, for I am a man of unclean lips, and I live among a people of unclean lips; yet my eyes have seen the King, the LORD of hosts!" (Isaiah 6:1, 5)

To really see God means that you are going to feel overwhelmed. This vision may generate intense affection and adoration, but the feeling may also prompt abject terror. The holiness of God is that stunning, as it certainly was for Isaiah and has been for other people of God, from Moses to Ezekiel, from Mary to John.

The posture of fear, awe, and reverence builds a highway from a vision of God's otherness to a life of humility and the pursuit of purity. The feeling of holy fear toward God corrects the casual ease expressed so often by those who see God simply as a distant force of niceness. And holy fear corrects the sheer contempt bred by familiarity with comfortable, self-congratulatory churchiness. Inducements toward and products generated by such fear, awe, and reverence come right from the first set of commandments:

> Then God spoke all these words:
> I am the LORD your God, who brought you out of the land of Egypt, out of the house of slavery; you shall have no other gods before me.
> You shall not make for yourself an idol, whether in the form of anything that is in heaven above, or that is on the earth beneath, or that is in the water under the earth. You shall not bow down to them or worship them; for I the LORD your God am a jealous God, punishing children for the iniquity of parents, to the third and the fourth generation of those who reject me, but showing steadfast love to the thousandth generation of those who love me and keep my commandments.
> You shall not make wrongful use of the name of the LORD your God, for the LORD will not acquit anyone who misuses his name. (Exod. 20:1–7)

Consider these commandments in sequence. First and foremost, I, the one who emancipated you, lay exclusive claim on you; you shall allow no other claimants to steal your allegiance away from me. Second, you shall not define me by creating an image, an analogy, or a characterization that shrinks me down to size. I am so far greater than anything you can think or imagine. You must not allow your limited mental capacity to limit who I am to categories of your own devising. Third, do not take lightly my name—Yahweh, the name above all names—whether used as a curse word or as a tool for making oaths. Don't use me for your own ends!

In each of these commands the holy otherness of God is elevated to a level far above our human capacity to understand. And with it comes a wholesale repudiation of any and all false gods to which people have been drawn—whether the religious gods of pagan deities or the distracting gods of money, sex, or power. From Aaron's molding of a golden calf at the foot of Mt. Sinai (Exod. 32) to the final dispatching of all idolaters into the lake of fire reported in the last pages of the New Testament (Rev. 21:8), idolatry is condemned wholesale.

This revulsion toward false gods surely stands as a major driver of the actions taken by the first apostolic council that gathered in Jerusalem (Acts 15). With quick dispatch the apostles were shrugging off the defining earmarks of their inherited covenantal faith: circumcision, Sabbath keeping, and keeping kosher. At least they were exempting their new Gentile converts from needing to subscribe to such practices. But they knew that there remained some nonnegotiables, some behaviors that cannot be countenanced in the community of faith. They delineated four prohibitions that Jesus' brother James summarized for the council of Jerusalem:

> "I have reached the decision that we should not trouble those Gentiles who are turning to God, but we should write to them to abstain only from things polluted by idols and from fornication and from whatever has been strangled and from blood. For in every city, for generations past, Moses has had those who proclaim him, for he has been read aloud every sabbath in the synagogues." (Acts 15:19–21)

What was the first prohibition? It was the one that honored the First Commandment: associating with false gods. Reflective of their context, that took the form of a prohibition against imbibing food "polluted by idols." For the new believers who resided in Gentile cities, such as Peter's converts in Caesarea, it was no small thing to abstain from food offered to idols—because most meat was used for idol worship prior to being sold to the public. The Christians resisting association with such idolatry had just one alternative place to purchase meat: at the local synagogue (the rabbis served the Jewish community as their butchers, thereby guaranteeing that the meat was kosher).

The early Christians wanted to disassociate from idolatry and were keenly resisting any compromise. The sin lists of Paul and Peter consistently list idolatry as an evil to deplore (1 Cor. 6:9–10; Gal. 5:20; Eph. 5:5; Col. 3:5; 1 Pet. 4:3). Paul even commands the believers to disassociate from idolaters (1 Cor. 5:11). The standard persisted through the apostolic era, as evidenced by John's scolding believers in the churches in Pergamum and Thyatira (Rev. 2:14, 20), written well after the deaths of the other apostles.

Accordingly, the benchmark for fearing and revering God is to abstain from all false gods and from all alliances, behaviors, and associations that stand in competition for the allegiance we should have with God. Churches through the centuries have pressed their members to name and confess as alien any alliances that could be categorized as idols lest we believers get caught in their webs. Then again, realistic about human waywardness, they have applied the abstinence standard by calling their members to take a fearless moral inventory—to confess as sin all such alliances whenever gathering together for worship of the one, true God.

However, into this clear, single-minded pattern of devotion the apostle Paul throws a caveat of hand-grenade proportions. He equivocates on the issue. When addressing the matter in Corinth—in the same letter that twice speaks against associating with idolatry and idolaters—he seems to back away from such an absolute position.

He starts by commanding them, consistent with the other commands referenced above, "Therefore, my dear friends, flee from the worship of idols" (1 Cor. 10:14). But then he qualifies the matter by declaring that the food will not harm them; that what's at stake is the impression being made on others that they are participating in and, therefore, giving their approval to the worship of idols (1 Cor. 10:19–22).

"Eat whatever is sold in the meat market without raising any questions on the ground of conscience, for 'the earth and its fullness are the Lord's'" (1 Cor. 10:25, 26). What he does not say is what he and the Corinthians know, that their city was one of the most pagan in the region. All of the meat sold in the Corinth meat markets came from the pagan temples. Animals were presented to the pagan priests to offer to the pagan gods worshiped there and were then sold in the market for the temple's profit. The synagogue in town provided kosher meat for Jews and Christians, but no pagan would be shopping there.

Accordingly, when invited to eat in the homes of the pagans, they knew where the meat came from, and that presented a moral dilemma: Should they refuse the idol-offered meat on the grounds that doing so would compromise their faith? If they do so, they'll be insulting their host. Or should they eat the meat, knowing that idols are figments of people's imaginations and that by eating the meat they would avoid embarrassing or insulting their host? Paul responded to this dilemma by saying,

> If an unbeliever invites you to a meal and you are disposed to go, eat whatever is set before you without raising any question on the ground of conscience. But if someone says to you, "This has been offered in sacrifice," then do not eat it, out of consideration for the one who informed you, and for the sake of conscience—I mean the other's conscience, not your own. For why should my liberty be subject to the judgment of someone else's conscience? (1 Cor. 10:27–29)

In other words, "If they don't tell, you don't need to ask; enjoy the meal. If they do tell, that's because they are feeling awkward for putting you into a compromising situation; in that case, to relieve their awkwardness, say, 'No, thanks' for the meal." In Paul's view, the matter of idolatry is secondary to the matter of Christian witness. What sounds like an absolute prohibition actually comes across as a benchmark/standard that allows room for approximations and adjustments.

The First Israeli Idol

The New Testament's mixed messages regarding idolatry harken back to the first explicit participation in the practice: the forging of the golden calf at the foot of Mt. Sinai. The Israelites probably weren't trying to rebel against the very God whose plagues had delivered them from Egypt and whose parting of the waters had protected them from the attacking Egyptian soldiers. They likely were simply trying to form a representation of the God of power as a way to give homage, but that gesture wasn't well received by God or Moses.

We need to turn back a page or two, however, in the story. Where would these wilderness wanderers have found the gold with which to build this statue? Prior to leaving their slaveholders in Egypt, they were given the orders, and well they obeyed them, to "take the spoils of the Egyptians" (Exod. 3:22; 12:36). They thus left with their pocketbooks full.

So when Aaron called for them to share the wealth, they heartily presented their fair share. They were then punished for their idolatry when the Decalogue-toting Moses descended the mountain. After his second descent, he commanded the people to build God a traveling tent with beautiful furniture, including the ark of the covenant—to be made of pure gold. Where did they get that gold? From the same source as was used for the golden calf: the spoils of the Egyptians.

In fact, on many occasions through the biblical pages that follow, God's people took products and ideas from secular, even anti-God sources, and appropriated them for God. The Greek language that spread throughout the Mediterranean world during Alexander the Great's reign provided the means of communication used for the spread of the gospel. The extensive highway system built by the Romans provided the means by which the apostles took the gospel "to the uttermost parts of the earth" (Acts 1:8). And the *Pax Romana*, the peaceful stability built by Israel's oppressors and early Christianity's persecutors, provided the believers a safer context within which to spread far and wide the good news of their Savior and Lord.

The apostle Paul himself, when visiting in Athens, cites their statue to the "unknown god" as pointing to the God of Israel made known in Jesus Christ and sees it as a way to proclaim the gospel. He also cites a popular secular poet in order to slip his foot in the door of his audience's consciousness (see Acts 17:22–31).

Christians in mission have ever since "taken the spoils of the Egyptians"—appropriated languages, cultures, commodities, products, skills, talents, and you-name-it of secular and differently religious people in order to share God's word with them. So while it is generally good to disassociate from all idols, it is also good to associate with nonbelievers for the sake of giving a witness to them in word and deed about Jesus the Christ. If doing so means that you eat whatever they offer, go ahead, lest the food issues get in the way of the far more important issue: sharing the love of the Lord.

Doing Justice

When relating to the world, the effort to repurpose for God's sake matters of secular origin poses both wondrous possibilities and dangerous, unintended consequences. On the negative side, some matters cannot be repurposed. Sometimes taking the patient route or negotiating a peace with evildoers runs akin to the practice of appeasement, most often associated with Prime Minister Neville Chamberlain's concessions to Adolph Hitler from 1937–39. Such policy efforts only helped the evils of Nazi Germany to escalate.

Instead, another word jumps to center stage: *justice*. The prophet Micah's most famous words summarize God's expectations of us:

> He has told you, O mortal, what is good;
>> and what does the LORD require of you
> but to do justice, and to love kindness,
>> and to walk humbly with your God?
>>>> (Mic. 6:8)

Isaiah presses the same point with ferocity:

> Is not this the fast that I choose:
>> to loose the bonds of injustice,
>> to undo the thongs of the yoke,
> to let the oppressed go free,
>> and to break every yoke?
> Is it not to share your bread with the hungry,
>> and bring the homeless poor into your house;
> when you see the naked, to cover them,
>> and not to hide yourself from your own kin?
> Then your light shall break forth like the dawn,
>> and your healing shall spring up quickly;
> your vindicator shall go before you,
>> the glory of the LORD shall be your rear guard.
> Then you shall call, and the LORD will answer;
>> you shall cry for help, and he will say, Here I am.
>>>> (Isa. 58:6–9a)

The prophet's promises are composed of a poetry of sheer beauty, but those promises ring hollow if uttered apart from the prerequisites that surround them. In fact, Isaiah and other prophets of both testaments set the prerequisites in blunt terms: Do justice; break chains of injustice; liberate the oppressed; feed the hungry; clothe the naked; house the homeless.

My late scholar friend Arthur Baird took his PhD in New Testament in Scotland at the Free Church College (later renamed the Edinburgh Theological Seminary) at the University of Edinburgh. He kiddingly said that his dissertation was not by any stretch the best one ever submitted, but it was the longest ever allowed. It was around eight hundred pages on the topic "The Justice of God." Why did Baird have so much to say? Because the Bible says so much on the topic. While an English language concordance may not show as many references to "the justice of God," the Hebrew and Greek concordances show many more, given that *justice* often get translated as "righteousness."

The Greek word *dikaiosune* is mentioned eighty-five times in the New Testament, often to speak of a broad sense of goodness and rightness but also to speak of justice, or the practice of assuring that all persons get their due. The Hebrew words *mishpat*, meaning "treating people equitably," and *tsadekah*, meaning "obligatory sharing, fairness, and justice," together appear over 350 times in the Hebrew Scriptures. Both are expressed as commands to be pursued relentlessly, and hence, the pursuit of such justice is a central aspiration set before believers in the three major monotheistic faiths.

Treating people equitably, giving them their due, generally implies two kinds of fairness: one dealing legal justice on the innocent and guilty as deserved and the other assuring people of life's essential needs. The former focuses on law and punishment and can be categorized as disciplinary justice. The latter focuses on economics and human rights and can be categorized as distributive justice. To suggest that biblical justice includes both categories, however, is to incite political war. The two American political parties fly one flag or the other, with the one regularly promoting the strong arm of law and justice to protect the peace and the other advocating justice for those wronged by systems and structures that exclude and impoverish them. The former seeks to bring perpetrators to justice. The latter aims to bring justice to victims. Both kinds of justice are promoted, indeed required, in Scripture.

A process of disciplinary justice is spelled out in detail in Deuteronomy 16:18–21:23. It begins with a clear command to exercise integrity:

> You shall appoint judges and officials throughout your tribes, in all your towns that the LORD your God is giving you, and they shall render just decisions for the people. You must not distort justice; you must not show partiality; and

you must not accept bribes, for a bribe blinds the eyes of the
wise and subverts the cause of those who are in the right.
Justice, and only justice, you shall pursue, so that you may
live and occupy the land that the LORD your God is giving
you. (Deut. 16:18–20)

While the rules in that lengthy passage may seem to us antiquated
and overly punitive, still the point about fairness, judicial restraint,
and the rights of the accused are very modern.

Regarding disciplinary justice, Tim Keller explains, "It means
acquitting or punishing every person on the merits of the case,
regardless of race or social status. Anyone who does the same wrong
should be given the same penalty."[1] The exercise of distributive justice begins with the assumption that the human community func-
tions as a nuclear family writ large. As parents look after the welfare
of their children, so, too, the faith community looks after its children
and its extended family members:

There will, however, be no one in need among you, because
the LORD is sure to bless you in the land that the LORD your
God is giving you as a possession to occupy, if only you will
obey the LORD your God by diligently observing this entire
commandment that I command you today. (Deut. 15:4–5)

The actual implementation of this notion of sharing required the
emerging Israeli people to extend their notion of community beyond
not just one's own nuclear and extended family but also one's own
nation. It gets expressed in terms of agrarian economics in their
much-traveled region of the world (the land bridge between Europe/
Asia and Egypt/Africa). In anticipation of their move into the land of
Canaan, Moses commanded them, "When you reap the harvest of
your land, you shall not reap to the very edges of your field, or gather
the gleanings of your harvest; you shall leave them for the poor and
for the alien: I am the LORD your God" (Lev. 23:22).

A similar approach is commanded near the end of the Torah:

---

1. Tim Keller, "What Is Biblical Justice?" *Relevant Magazine*, Aug. 23, 2012,
http://www.relevantmagazine.com/god/practical-faith/what-biblical-justice.

> When you reap your harvest in your field and forget a sheaf in the field, you shall not go back to get it; it shall be left for the alien, the orphan, and the widow, so that the LORD your God may bless you in all your undertakings. When you beat your olive trees, do not strip what is left; it shall be for the alien, the orphan, and the widow.
>
> When you gather the grapes of your vineyard, do not glean what is left; it shall be for the alien, the orphan, and the widow. Remember that you were a slave in the land of Egypt; therefore I am commanding you to do this. (Deut. 24:19–22).

Such commands suggest that our sowing of seed, our investment of funds, and our exertion of energy in work is not only for self-preservation but also for the care and preservation of others. And those others include not just those in our immediate and extended family but those of the larger community—even strangers and aliens. Such a command presupposes the obligation to take responsibility for those in need and those lacking family or national status.

Such commands took on even greater economic impact in the Hebrew Scriptures with the instituting of the Sabbath laws—requiring that everybody, even the poor and immigrant laborers, enjoy at least one day of rest in each week. They also required that the land be allowed to rest one year in seven, and every seven-times-seven years a year of Jubilee was to be marked. On that fiftieth year, all debts were to be cancelled, all slaves were to be emancipated, and the whole nation was to share the bounty of the previous years' harvests.

A third category of justice, restorative justice, has emerged in Judeo-Christian circles as a particular application of distributive justice. It captures the notion of the Jubilee by requiring the privileged to assure that those who are exploited, neglected, denied, or deprived would be given back not only the rights denied them heretofore but also a reasonable path to gaining back what was taken from them. When rebuilding the nation, Nehemiah instituted the Jubilee laws not for fifty-year cycles but in the simple seven-year cycle: ". . . and we will forego the crops of the seventh year and the exaction of every debt" (Neh. 10:31).

Amid Israel's conflicts, the prophet Amos speaks out:

I hate, I despise your festivals,
    and I take no delight in your solemn assemblies.
Even though you offer me your burnt offerings and grain
       offerings,
    I will not accept them;
and the offerings of well-being of your fatted animals
    I will not look upon.
Take away from me the noise of your songs;
    I will not listen to the melody of your harps.
But let justice roll down like waters,
    and righteousness like an ever-flowing stream.

                                         (Amos 5:21–24)

Helen Keller summarized such justice well: "Until the great mass of the people shall be filled with the sense of responsibility for each other's welfare, social justice can never be attained."

Jesus also said it clearly, as reported by Luke:

> "There is one thing lacking. Sell all that you own and distribute the money to the poor, and you will have treasure in heaven; then come, follow me." When he heard this, he became sad, for he was very rich. Jesus looked at him and said, "How hard it is for those who have wealth to enter the kingdom of God! Indeed, it is easier for a camel to go through the eye of a needle than for someone who is rich to enter the kingdom of God." (Luke 18:22–25)

From Benchmarks to Adaptations

Most twenty-first-century people live in contexts quite dissimilar from those of the agrarian, nomadic tribes of ancient Israel. Still, the aspiration to treat others equitably leads us to affirm the essential benchmarks found in the Bible: Do justice, and break the chains of injustice. Similarly, we are called on to move from benchmarks to applications: to exercise distributive and disciplinary justice and to promote just social structures.

As it is, the world created by the Lord of justice has within it many evidences of the common grace of God: the ability of societies to govern themselves and to develop mechanisms of commerce that give rise to tides that lift up all of the boats. But just as evident are the corruptions of sinners' exploitations and the revamping of such systems in ways that serve their own selfish interests. As citizens of earthly kingdoms—national, regional, and local—we are granted mechanisms of influence ranging from writing letters to the editor to casting our votes in elections, from running for office to staging public protests, from teaching social studies classes to choosing companies in which to invest in stocks and bonds.

We can influence the systems and structures of society to promote justice or erode it. In their better moments, churches, synagogues, and mosques all have aligned themselves with God's justice by promoting institutions of society that promote the greater good for all. May such better moments multiply in our day.

Approximating and Adapting Justice

When considering the best ways to promote justice, one can easily lose perspective, either by being too uncompromising or too sympathetic. As it has evolved through the centuries, the effective exercise of disciplinary justice has left much latitude to the judges and juries as to how they punish guilty parties. Every story has a subplot; every situation is different; and every perpetrator is motivated in particular ways. Accordingly, the exacting process of taking "an eye for an eye, and a tooth for a tooth" while fair on the surface, sometimes ought to give way to mercy, leniency, and even clemency. The obvious case of the parent stealing a loaf of bread to feed the hungry child does not match the case of the thief stealing diamonds from a jewelry store. Approximations and adaptations of such kinds certainly are in store.

When exercising distributive and restorative justice, one can easily take actions that seem noble but actually exacerbate a situation. As urban activist Robert Lupton has reported in his book *Toxic Charity*, much charitable and missional service actually harms the persons it is aiming to help[2]. Too often noble efforts turn the less fortunate into objects of pity, which diminishes their dignity. In turn, it robs

---

2. Robert D. Lupton, *Toxic Charity: How Churches and Charities Hurt Those They Help (and How to Reverse It)* (New York: One, 2011).

them of their work ethic, generating increased dependency on others' generosity.

While charity and generosity of all kinds are always good values to cultivate, just as are the breaking of chains of injustice, the follow-through on such efforts requires careful consideration, judicious study, and an eye toward empowering individuals and communities to become more self-sustaining, self-sufficient, and self-motivated. Hence, even doing justice requires room for approximating and adapting.

In the World but Not of It

When considering how to repurpose secular resources for God's service—"taking the spoils of the Egyptians"—and exercising justice, we are ultimately asking just how people of faith should relate to the world systems around them. Jesus addressed the question in this high priestly prayer:

> "I have given them your word, and the world has hated them because they do not belong to the world, just as I do not belong to the world. I am not asking you to take them out of the world, but I ask you to protect them from the evil one. They do not belong to the world, just as I do not belong to the world. Sanctify them in the truth; your word is truth. As you sent me into the world, I have sent them into the world." (John 17:14–18).

Along that vein Paul exhorted the Roman Christians, "Do not be conformed to this world, but be transformed by the renewing of your minds, so that you may discern what is the will of God—what is good and acceptable and perfect" (Rom. 12:2).

So how can we be in the world but not of it? Perhaps H. Richard Niebuhr explained it best in his brief but profound book *Christ and Culture*,[3] where he posits several ways to relate to the world. Some treat Christ as "against" the culture. Others see Christ as "of" the

---

3. H. Richard Niebuhr, *Christ and Culture* (New York: Harper & Brothers, 1951), chap. 4.

culture—indistinguishable from it. Some treat Christ as "above" culture and live very separated lives. Some see Christ as operating in paradox with the culture—leading to a "both-and" relationship. Still others see Christ as "transforming" culture.

Niebuhr does not maintain that only one of these is correct, but it's not hard to infer that the latter is the primary way he recommends. Same here. To be in but not of the world is to be one who has the courage to name injustices for what they are and to boldly break such chains in order to liberate others to become their best selves, all the while seeking to give others their due. Still, such justice promotion is tempered by the approximating and adapting required by extending, as much as possible, not the clenched fist of judgment but the open hand of mercy. At the same time it seeks to empower personal growth in place of enabling dependency in others.

Such a transforming relationship with the culture entails the need to aspire to a life of uncompromised reverence for the holy God—and with that, a repudiation of all things evil. Still, it also looks for ways to repurpose secularly developed commodities, skills, and resources into tools for God's use so that God may be magnified and God's purposes realized in this life and in this world.

One key element not highlighted sufficiently so far begs for more consideration: How do we pursue godly aspirations, formulate benchmarks/standards, articulate regular applications, and discern an appropriate range of approximations and adaptations as we live this life out in our communities? What role do others play to help us discern the right from the wrong, and how do we engage with others in their and our shared decision making? To those questions we turn next.

6

Discerning God's Will
As If It Matters to Others
As Much As It Does to You

Before proceeding, let's recap a bit. What we have been trying to do from the opening page has been to ask how best we can make good choices from among the many options that present themselves on any given day. We want to make such choices because we know that it's better to be good than to be bad—even though some kinds of performances, social settings, and personal interactions may playfully romanticize "being bad." We want to do right by people, and we want to walk uprightly before God.

Accordingly, we resonate with Jesus' words drawn from the Hebrew Scriptures that he dubs the Great Commandment: Love the Lord your God with all of your heart, all of your soul, all of your mind, and all of your strength; and love your neighbor as yourself (see Matt. 22:37–39; Mark 12:29–31; Luke 10:25–28). We also know that each of these two life-guiding principles begs for more specificity. We spelled that out by way of listing sets of aspirations—seven virtues for each of the two guiding principles—that persons of earnestness strive to apply and achieve.

Then again, those aspirations themselves look for visible, tangible, and measureable ways to be put into action. The Scriptures provide corresponding standards, which give us benchmarks against which we can measure options and possible adjustments. They, in turn, have generated particular ways of being applied in our communities of faith and geography, hence the term *applications*. These vary somewhat from one faith community to another, from one ethnic community to another, and from one region to another.

While holding onto these two life principles, their enumerated aspirations, standards/benchmarks, and applications, we can't help but note that in the biblical record, in personal intuition, and in community practice we all give allowance to approximations and adaptations. We all stretch, bend, and reformulate some practices in the spirit of the aspirations while not quite matching the more exacting standards/benchmarks and regularized applications that we still affirm in principle.

Have you read yourself into any of the categories of decision making we have outlined so far? Many who have sat through lectures on this subject have said, "You're telling my story" or "That's just how I make decisions. I've just never thought of it in this way." How about you? Well, in this chapter you may find a part of the decision-making process that you do not naturally follow. You may not relate to it easily at all. If you are an American, like I am, there is a high likelihood that you don't do much decision making in your community. But that makes this chapter all the more important.

The American Way

I love being an American. One thing my national heritage has built into the core of my being is the instinct toward rugged individualism. To be free to choose one's path in life, one's vocation, and one's location and, for the most part, to be able to reap the full benefits of my labors: such privileges and pursuits have made me much of who I am. But I'm also cognizant of the flaws my American values have built into me, and one of the worst of them is my rugged individualism. I all too easily forget that my path in life, my choice of vocation, my location, and the opportunity to benefit from my labors have all been shaped, empowered, and facilitated by others. The community of family, church, government, and culture have contributed even more to who I am than I have.

And when it comes to making decisions, I do not make mine in a void. I do not stand alone. Whatever I decide today will impact others around me. If I gamble my money away, my spouse and children suffer the consequences. If I lose control of my car and run head on into another vehicle, I injure, maim, or even kill another. If, as a pastor, I preach boring sermons that put people to sleep, I convey to the worshipers that God is boring—a very false image!

Indeed, I type the letters on each page of this manuscript knowing without doubt that those who teach the faith will be held to a higher standard of judgment. I share my thoughts with you in fear and trembling, knowing that these ideas are not just my own ruminations; they are words purporting to represent God's word, and I shudder to think that anything I am writing may miss the mark. You see, while I am a ruggedly individualistic American, I am also a follower of Jesus and, as such, a member of the body of Christ, the family of God, the temple of the Holy Spirit. I am a part of Christian community, and "we're in it together," as says the well-worn phrase.

Christian Community Perception

Still, I am an American raised in the mentality Barry Schwartz calls the "official dogma of all Western industrial societies."[1] If we want to maximize the welfare of all our citizens, the official dogma says that we need to maximize individual freedom. Those who adhere to the official dogma argue that since freedom is in and of itself good, valuable, worthwhile, and essential to being human, then if we all have freedom, then we can all act on our own to do the things that will maximize our welfare. That way no one has to decide things on our behalf. Schwartz takes exception to that point, showing that the multiplication of choices in life has actually brought more frustration and paralysis than real freedom.

We can add that the church's continuing struggle to resist being held captive to its surrounding culture usually disregards this addiction to individualism. Like the fish swimming in the proverbial water, individualism is so ubiquitous, so pervasive, and so little challenged

---

1. Barry Schwartz, *The Paradox of Choice*, Ted Talks, July, 2005, http://www.ted.com/talks/barry_schwartz_on_the_paradox_of_choice#t-56861; also cited by Chris Higgins, "Barry Schwartz: The Paradox of Choice," mental_floss, http://mentalfloss.com/article/29030/barry-schwartz-paradox-choice.

that most of us Americans can't think outside the casket it has built around us (to mix metaphors).

One other reason to take exception to the "official dogma" is that it makes us stupid. If left to myself, my ability to discern right from wrong, God's will from my own, gets blinded by a subjectivism from which there is no escape. No matter how noble I may think myself to be, I cannot escape myself, my self-centeredness, my self-serving instincts unless an outside force shines its own light on my questions and posited solutions. I need others' help to discern God's will. John Calvin himself spoke of the noetic effects of sin (from the Greek word *noetikos*, "intellect"), stating that the presence and practice of sin blinds the mind from perceiving truth clearly if it is not illuminated by the Holy Spirit.

Yes, we need the help of the Holy Spirit to help us see better. And the Holy Spirit most often speaks through sources outside of ourselves: the Bible; other readings; lectures and sermons; and the council of wise friends, beloved family members, and even systems and structures of society—ranging from a prayer group, Sunday school class, and church community to an arresting officer, prosecutor, judge, and jury. We need people in our lives who will speak the truth to us—hopefully in love.

Around the dinner table, a family plans a vacation, decides to invite friends over, or talks about the possibility of moving or taking a new job. Around the board room, the elders or deacons of the church assess the congregation's next steps in outreach, Christian education, mission giving, and pastoral care. In the voting booth, the community elects their next mayor, governor, or president. So many discernment questions involve the communities in which we are members . . . all the way to the kingdom of God itself.

Been Here. Done This.

We have talked about the role of community in the discerning and implementing process, and when speaking of the guiding principle of loving God, we spoke of our aspiration to glorify God and said that the central means of doing so is to join with others in worship. We have also talked about the aspiration to adore God, highlighting the regular practice of group prayer to help in the adoration, and we spoke of the aspiration to put on the mind of Christ. Few methods are as pivotal in accomplishing that as participating in a Bible study group. Finally, we shared the aspiration to take up our cross to follow Christ—highlighting that the servant spirit needs to become tangible by way of church discipline and the exercise of mutual accountability.

All of these aspirations require us to participate in Christian community. Specific to community is that very word *accountability* just mentioned. To be accountable requires the general state of engaging in relationships with others. A spirit of submission is necessary— not blind obedience, and certainly not obedience in all matters, but a willingness to be questioned, challenged, and tested. Those who have found a fellowship of such openness, vulnerability, and candor often witness that it has become their lifeline. And they have found that it has swung open a door into a much clearer discernment of God's will in their lives.

The same goes for all of the ways we have spoken about loving neighbors. Whenever we aim to fulfill the neighborly aspirations, to articulate the corresponding standards/benchmarks, to summarize the applications, and to wrestle with possible approximations and adaptations, our best chance of moving effectively comes from operating in community with others.

Complexity of Community

The significance of community is still bigger than the practical benefits outlined above. The community's role in helping discern God's will has pivotal impact, even in the most nuanced and complex decisions to be made—when we allow it to do so. But what do we mean by "community"? The community of the faithful has three interactive and interdependent groupings. For our purposes we'll call them 1) microcommunity, 2) congregational community, and 3) metacommunity.

The microcommunity usually takes the form of a household, such as a nuclear family. It may be supplemented or supplanted by another small grouping (less than a dozen members), such as a support group, a prayer group, a study group, and/or an accountability group. Healthy microcommunities are marked by high disclosure, candid critique, and a one-for-all-and-all-for-one loyalty.

A congregational community typically ranges from 25 to 25,000 in number (most between 25 and 1,000—except for Roman Catholic parishes and megachurches). It has a leader or leaders, worshipful rituals, shared convictions, and missional purpose. Unlike in a micro-community, active members may not know all of the other members or even a majority of them, but they do share a common identity with one another.

A metacommunity is a far broader and diverse self-defining group numbering from thousands to hundreds of millions, yet it still has defining characteristics for its members. Most call themselves a denomination or association. Some are quite homogeneous in form and content; others allow wide ranges of ideas and practices. Or, hearkening back to the terms we have been using, all Christians affirm the primary principles to love God and neighbor; most are seeking to fulfill the fourteen aspirations; and most would also recognize the standards as benchmarks, although with some variations on those themes. The points of application would be recognized by most as being historic, but these communities would show their own distinctive characteristics.

Regardless of how much these communities vary, decisions are not made within a void. Members decide together, informed and influenced by their faith communities, and their decisions give new shape to those respective communities.

And as members of a faith community facing difficult choices, we can be true to ourselves only while engaging with each of the microcommunities, congregational communities, and metacommunities that have shaped our identities. Granted, we can criticize our own communities' myopia—our collective subjectivism, prejudices, idiosyncrasies, and stultifying traditionalism. But we still need to honor our capital-*T* Tradition if only by studying its historic missions, visions, and modi operandi, so as to be best informed when deciding whether we will reaffirm, approximate, or adapt it—or maybe even try to change it wholesale for others' sakes.

One other comment—which may appear almost too obvious to state—is that the richest experience of community is enjoyed best by those who identify closely with all three of these concentric circles. They know intimately those in their microcommunity. They relate and carry out the rituals intrinsic to their congregational community.

And they identify regionally, nationally, and, if possible, internationally with their metacommunity. This doesn't make for an alternate Trinity, but the language of "three-in-one" does fit here.

Freedom of the Conscience

One's relationship to one's three communities often arises in the context of questions regarding conscience. Thomas Aquinas famously said, "Every judgment of conscience, be it right or wrong, be it about things evil in themselves or morally indifferent, is obligatory, in such that he who acts against his conscience always sins."[2]

Martin Luther took exception to some of the ideas of Thomas's Roman Catholic church, but he spoke similarly about the conscience: "Justice is a temporary thing that must at last come to an end; but the conscience is eternal and will never die."[3]

Vatican II expanded Thomas's perspective:

> In the depths of his conscience man detects a law which he does not impose on himself, but which holds him to obedience. Always summoning him to love good and avoid evil, the voice of conscience can when necessary speak to his heart more specifically: do this, shun that. For man has in his heart a law written by God. To obey it is the very dignity of man; according to it he will be judged (cf. Rom. 2:14–16).[4]

And just a few years later, amid the civil rights efforts in the United States, Martin Luther King Jr. penned the following in his "Letter from a Birmingham Jail":

> An individual who breaks a law that conscience tells him is unjust and who willingly accepts the penalty of imprisonment in order to arouse the conscience of the community

2. Thomas, Aquinas, *III Quodlibet* (1270), question 27.

3. Martin Luther, "On Marriage," 1530, Wikiquote, https://en.wikiquote.org/wiki/Martin_Luther.

4. Pope Paul VI, *Pastoral Constitution on the Church in the Modern World, Gaudium et Spes*, December 6, 1965 (Boston: St. Pauls Books & Media), 16.

over its injustice, is in reality expressing the highest respect for the law.[5]

However, Thomas did not think of conscience merely through the eyes of rugged individualism. He shaped the metachurch tradition of Catholicism and formulated the catechetical teaching to help shape its adherents' convictions about right and wrong. Martin Luther promoted freedom of the conscience, urging all believers to read the Scriptures for themselves; yet he, too, added thousands of pages of commentary, theological analysis, and ethical formulations to help congregants to better understand holy writ. Vatican II presented a host of church teachings on conscience, and Martin Luther King Jr. urged the nation to write laws to set requirements for the proper forming of the conscience.

The exercise of the conscience and the discernment of God's will in Christian community have been complicated. Still, those efforts cannot be abandoned. Conscience can and must operate within a "community of character," as Stanley Hauerwas has outlined.[6] The experience of living in these kinds of communities has generated for all persons a narrative of shared understandings that has shaped us into who we are, and when we face difficult questions, it behooves us to be informed by those communities.

For persons of faith, those communities have formed the value systems we have been summarizing in this book—the guiding principles, aspirations (akin to the virtues ethics outlined in Hauerwas), standards/benchmarks, and applications.

Conscientious Objection

However, if we return to the quote above by Martin Luther King Jr. in his "Letter from Birmingham Jail," times do arise when a person feels compelled to break "a law that conscience tells him is unjust." What then? Historically, the Protestant principle has argued for

5. Martin Luther King Jr., "From the Birmingham Jail," *Christian Century* 80 (June 12, 1963): 767–73.

6. Stanley Hauerwas, *A Community of Character: Toward a Constructive Christian Social Ethic* (Notre Dame, IN: Notre Dame Press, 1981).

following conscience and being willing to pay the price. The judgment of the conscience has been treated as sacrosanct. Indeed, the Westminster Confession of Faith spells it out:

> God alone is Lord of the conscience, and hath left it free from the doctrines and commandments of men which are in anything contrary to his Word, or beside it in matters of faith and worship. So that to believe such doctrines, or to obey such commandments out of conscience, is to betray true liberty of conscience; and the requiring an implicit faith, and an absolute and blind obedience, is to destroy liberty of conscience, and reason also.[7]

Of course, in Westminster style, a string of caveats follows: disqualifying any practice of sin, disobeying lawful powers, promoting or practicing actions contrary to nature or known principles of Christianity, or destroying the peace. Still, the Protestant principle of giving all of one's allegiance to God and God alone has generated a culture of disregard toward the tradition, toward the metacommunity of the faithful.

The Informed Conscience

While the Roman Catholic tradition has been accused of shunning all free exercise of conscience, it actually pulls together freedom from and respect toward the metacommunity. Ask any good Roman Catholic priest-theologian about the "informed conscience," and he is likely to say that it is widely and wildly misunderstood. To be sure, many a Roman Catholic has never heard of the expression, and many of those who have heard of it have taken it to mean something far removed from actual church policy.

Yes, many Catholics assume that church law—like the prohibition against using artificial forms of birth control—must be followed at all times and that those failing to do so are excommunicated without

---

7. *The Constitution of the Presbyterian Church (U.S.A.)*, Part I, *Book of Confessions* (Louisville, KY: Office of the General Assembly, Presbyterian Church (U.S.A.), 1999), 6.109.

recourse. Then again, other Catholics have heard of "informed conscience" and interpreted it as license to follow their consciences on the assumption that they are already well-formed and informed.

On the contrary, the expression calls for a process of study to cultivate an informed conscience that can then lead to a conscientious and respected act of ecclesiastical disobedience, allowing one's church membership to remain secure. Imagine a newlywed Roman Catholic couple that discovers that one of them has a genetic condition that leads to a high likelihood of major disabilities to any child that they might bear. They follow their doctor's advice and begin using birth control pills, but they recognize the disconnect, even hypocrisy, between that practice and their faith. So they visit their parish priest, who reviews the church's policy and encourages them to trust in God to bless them with healthy children. He also warns them that they are acting in ways contrary to the vows they made months earlier when he prepared them for their wedding and that they are in violation of church policy.

The couple's familiarity with the dangers leads them to say, "We appeal the church's ruling on the basis of an informed conscience." The priest pauses, takes a deep breath, and says, "Okay, time for some study." He presents a plan for shared study that could take a few months. He gives them a book list, assigns a book a week, and sets a schedule of weekly conferences with him to discuss the week's reading. They follow through with him step-by-step, reading texts ranging from Aristotle to Aquinas, Newman to John Paul II. Week by week they discuss the readings, summarize what they have gained, and share what insights they have gleaned. Finally, at their final session, the priest asks them to summarize all they have learned and to share their analysis of their options in the light of it all.

With clarity and acuity they answer all of his questions. Finally he asks them, "Then in the light of your informed conscience, and in the light of the church's teachings, what do you believe to be the right thing for you to do?" They respond, "Father, in the light of our informed consciences, in the light of the teachings of the church, we believe that the right, responsible, and faithful thing to do is to avoid becoming pregnant. We believe that we should continue taking birth control, and we would like to continue to maintain our standing as full members of this parish and of the Roman Catholic Church."

He responds, "Well, as you can imagine, I don't believe that you are drawing the best final conclusion, but I do recognize that you have applied yourselves diligently to inform your consciences. You have studied the church's teachings on related subjects to an extensive degree, and I thereby grant you absolution for proceeding according to your conscience. Your membership remains intact. I'll be looking for you at mass on Sunday, so I can serve you Holy Communion."[8]

The "informed conscience," following Roman Catholic policy and practice, is thus one that affirms the freedom of the conscience and entrusts a person with the obligation to obey her or his conscience. But it also informs the person's conscience in respect of and in solidarity with one's microcommunity, congregational community, and metacommunity. The Tradition is honored even as it is disobeyed in a conscientious way. Or as Martin Luther King Jr. put it, such an act of breaking a law that conscience declares to be unjust "is in reality expressing the highest respect for the law."[9]

A House Undivided

While it is true that Jesus said that a house divided against itself cannot stand, still a house that allows for conscientious objections to actions can stand tall when handled with this kind of integrity. In the informed-conscience process outlined above, several outcomes all stand together:

- The person(s) facing a difficult dilemma gets to walk through it not in isolation—which is usually the case in high-conformity, shame-generating faith communities—but with the support of a loving faith community.
- This process allows the person(s) to engage in study with a church that has prepared itself for times of disagreement and sees such times as ripe for disciple formation.
- The process is engaged not in a hurry but over time, requiring effort, study, and open, candid dialogue.

8. For another example of an informed-conscience exchange between priest and parishioner, in this case dealing with end-of-life issues, see Richard M. Gula, SS, *Moral Discernment* (Mahwah, NJ: Paulist Press, 1997), 120–30.

9. King, "Letter from Birmingham Jail."

- This process allows for disagreement on the matter at hand but only after pursuing every opportunity to find agreement; it also agrees that at the heart of the matter the persons share their church's faith and share a commitment to love God and love one another. To "agree to disagree" results not as a flip, trivial response but as one forged in the heat of intense discussion.
- The church's policies on the matter remain in place; the resulting action of the individuals does not set a precedent for others to follow willy-nilly.
- The dissenter's choice is to depart from such policies without facing prosecution-unto-excommunication.

For the Rest of Us

Lest we miss the obvious implications, the rest of the Christian, Jewish, and Muslim worlds have much to learn from their Roman Catholic sisters and brothers. We have a long way to go to become communities of character or, perhaps better put, communities of informed consciences. For one thing, we need to save ourselves from being communities of political-party affiliation. As long as we are so easily pegged by our party platforms and ideologies—which always meld high principles with politicians' own self-promotion and other self-serving moral trade-offs—nobody with a dissenting position will muster the courage to ask for help to inform his or her own conscience.

It's going to take a far more integrative Christian ethic, drawn from Scripture and informed by two millennia of learning from mistakes, to help us all develop the kinds of informed consciences that Scripture and the church have been equipped to do. Then again, the Roman Catholic world would do well to advertise better the fact that they stand ready to help their members grow in their own integrity, their own discernment, and their own ability to understand God's will. And all rugged American individuals would do well to reclaim their identity as a community of faith—what is variously called in Christian, Trinitarian terms the body of Christ, the family of God, and the temple of the Holy Spirit.

7

Matters of Life and Death

If only you'd known Ginger. The one person above all who prompted the writing of this book is Ginger. I met her in 1984 shortly after being ordained and installed into the pastorate of Trinity Presbyterian Church in Satellite Beach, Florida. She was a petite, ninety-pound, elderly widow, although her petite size and red hair made her look about twenty years younger than her age. My wife, Barbie, and I visited her in her home a few months after my arrival at the church. We hit it off quickly, and Barbie and I felt a kinship to her.

About three years into that pastorate, as the congregation was warming up to what we called "pre-service praise," a sing-along that I led from the piano, the bright flashing lights of an ambulance shot through the glass doors on the south side of the sanctuary. I tried not to show alarm, but my focus on the lyrics was distracted. As we continued, an usher walked up the side aisle to the chancel, cupped his hand around my ear, and whispered, "It's Ginger. She fell."

I gasped but continued to play. When the song ended, I continued playing the piano softly and led the congregation in prayer for Ginger, providing both an explanation for the outside commotion and doing the one thing we knew we could do: pray for God to help our beloved member.

After the worship service, I headed over to the hospital, marched to the intensive care unit, and found her body heaving as a respirator was blowing air in and drawing it out of her lungs. "This is more serious that I'd imagined," I whispered to myself. The nurse, realizing that I was her pastor, clued me in. She had nearly died and might not make it. Her brainwave activity was low, and she was being kept alive only by the respirator. They had called her son Brian, who would be there the next morning around 11 o'clock.

I had met Brian once before. A young Naval officer, he was stationed at Pearl Harbor in Honolulu. I now found myself dreading this next encounter with him. I hardly slept that night. What will I say to him? I wondered, Surely I should advise him and the doctors to do all they can to revive Ginger. That's the Christian thing to do, isn't it? The suggestion that humans could accelerate death was unthinkable to those of us who identified as pro-life. And at that time, the possibility of allowing even passive euthanasia was a matter fought in the courts and settled in favor of keeping people alive as God would certainly intend.

I'd discussed the matter theoretically a bit in my seminary education, all leading to a unanimous conclusion: God orders our days; God calls us home when God is ready; who are we to play God by terminating a human life? But the vision of Ginger's tubed arms, masked face, and machine-induced, expanding-and-contracting chest hardly struck me as anything that could be classified as natural or God-designed. And when I called into the ICU unit that evening and was told that she was now 80 percent brain dead, my simple life-and-death categories blurred.

The next morning, I ran by the church office to attend to a few administrative matters. While there, Ginger's best friend called to say that she now had less than 10 percent brainwave activity. I felt my own lungs empty as I knew that my young pastoral aptitude was about to face its toughest test to date. At 9:30 I headed over to the hospital to be sure to arrive well ahead of Ginger's son.

Creation Mandate, Dominion Covenant

A mile or so into the fifteen-minute ride to the hospital, a Scripture verse crossed my mind: "Be fruitful and multiply, and fill the earth and subdue it" (Gen. 26:28). These are the first words from God to a human recorded in the Bible (expressed to the solitary existing human, as the subject of a suitable partner had not yet been introduced).

I had studied this Scripture text at length in seminary under the labels "creation mandate" and "dominion covenant." I knew it to be a defining text in the development of the Protestant Reformation, one the *sola scriptura* Reformers used as proof positive that humans are not solely obedient to natural law, a point of departure from the Roman Church. This teaching of obedience to natural law had, in part, prompted the antiscientific Middle Ages. But with the Reformation came the assertion that humans are free to work and rework the natural world. Those scholars five centuries back ended up launching the modern scientific era, the rationalist movement, and the industrial revolution. Such freedom to experiment with and employ nature gave extra impetus to the rising Renaissance.

The creation-dominion theme drives the whole first chapter of Genesis, wherein on the first three days God creates the essential elements, and on the second three days God creates entities to rule over those elements. That is, the first day's light and darkness get ruled by the fourth day's sun, moon, and stars; the second day's sky and sea get ruled by the fifth day's birds and fish; the third day's land gets ruled by the sixth day's animals and, especially, the human(s)— all culminating in God instituting the dominion covenant with that first human.

But now, as that verse crossed my mind, I heard something more: God delegated to the first human the obligation and authority even of creating life—human life—itself. In other words, God told a human being to now do the very thing God has done: to create and order life. God commissioned humanity to play God, or something akin to that.

Be Fruitful . . . and Subdue

By the end of the second mile of my hospital run, I also latched onto the four imperatives God laid on that human. The first, second, and third all made the same point: generate life. The fourth, outnumbered by the other three, also gave the authority to "subdue it," that is, to take control over life, perhaps even to end it.

For better and for worse, my mind jumped to some of the more troubling passages of Scripture. I thought about the many orders given Moses on Mount Sinai that included the imposition of capital punishment for certain behaviors, some of which would not rise to the level of what my country's courts would ever have categorized as felonies or, much less, capital crimes.

I also knew from Bible study of instances during the conquest of Canaan when God apparently told the Israelites to kill their enemies—even, on occasion, the women, children, and animals. I had read and heard winsome sermons expounding young David's murderous duel with the giant Goliath.

Frankly, I reminded myself that the very term "sanctity of life"—one we pro-life Protestants had incorporated into our ecclesiastical vocabulary from our Roman Catholic friends—treats as absolute, totally sacred, what Scripture treats as something to be honored and valued but not to the level of absolute sacredness. Yes, life is valued highly but not to the level of the divine. God alone is sacred, holy, absolute.

But as this seminal verse of Scripture from Genesis rolled around in my mind, I couldn't help but think, "So who gave us the right to play God? God did! God gave us the right to play God." I was strangely comforted, yet at the same time my fear spiked even higher. "Oh my," I thought, "I'm going to have to help decide if Ginger should live or die." My thoughts were going at NASCAR speeds. I thought about other life-and-death choices that impose themselves on us. International conflicts on a level akin to but far exceeding the scale and scope of ancient Israel's battles. Capital crimes as handled in our modern courts. Problem pregnancies. Self-defense and, especially, the defense of innocent, helpless targets of armed assailants.

Choosing Life

A few more miles into that hospital drive there flashed before me a spreadsheet. No, not the sheet of unclean animals descending from heaven for groggy apostle Peter's viewing (Acts 10). But a spreadsheet—like the engineers in my church would fill out and bring to board meetings to overview the budget or plan the next year's calendar. Hearkening back to my high school days of making x–y charts in algebra and geometry, I listed in an initial left column five different categories of life-and-death decisions we humans have to address:

- Self-defense
- International conflict
- Crime and punishment
- Problem pregnancies
- Deteriorating health

I then thought of those three commands to that first human to generate life, and it was clear that each of these life-and-death decisions leant itself to a corresponding generate-life decision; they popped into a second column.

- When attacked, turn the other cheek, as Jesus said. When the stakes are high, run! Get away. Avoid the conflict so that nobody gets hurt.
- In matters of international disagreement, make peace quickly with your opponent—also a command of Jesus. Negotiate. Negotiate. Negotiate. Pursue all possible means to avoid taking up arms.
- When a person commits a crime, pursue a just prosecution (carefully gathering evidence), allow the accused to face the accusers and to present a defense, and if found guilty by a just court, let that person pay for the crimes via incarceration and restitution. Always aim to bring reconciliation and rehabilitation. Indeed, the very redemption central to Jesus' life and death could only seek such ends.
- So, too, when a woman is found to be with child—unintended, unplanned, frightful, community-shaming, poverty-inducing, boyfriend-denying, health-threatening—the best and most honorable thing would be to carry the child to term. Deliver the innocent child into the world to live a full life. If need be, place the child up for adoption.
- And in the case of a person suffering a life-threatening injury or disease, do all possible via prayer and medical means to

> bring the person back to health. If unable to do so, at least
> provide medications, support, and tender love to help the
> person die in dignity—in God's time.

All of these answers seemed in my mind to match the words recorded in the book of Deuteronomy:

> I call heaven and earth to witness against you today that
> I have set before you life and death, blessings and curses.
> Choose life so that you and your descendants may live, loving
> the LORD your God, obeying him, and holding fast to him;
> for that means life to you and length of days, so that you may
> live in the land that the LORD swore to give to your ancestors
> to Abraham, to Isaac, and to Jacob." (Deut. 30:19–20)

Now choose life. So be it.

But Ginger's situation wasn't exactly a textbook case on how to choose life. I was no neurologist, but I did know that dead brain cells do not regenerate. And I knew that the extension of life via mechanical tools went beyond the bounds of medical support that the doctors of Jesus' day would have been able to provide. This was an extraordinary situation, I surmised, and extraordinary times do call for extraordinary measures.

Extraordinary Times . . . Extraordinary Measures

I thought about the matter of self-defense. What if the person attacking you is intending and able to kill you? What if you can't run away? What if, indeed, the attack is not against you but against your adolescent daughter, or your toddler son, or your disabled neighbor, or any other helpless innocent bystander? What if the only possible option to save a life is to fight back, even to the possible conclusion of killing that person?

Civil laws would declare you innocent on the grounds of self-defense. And no church—not even the peace churches (such as Quakers and Mennonites) would excommunicate you for doing so. Extraordinary circumstances could lead to an ethical decision to end a life. A grievous decision to be sure, but a grievous ethical decision nonetheless. A third and a fourth column popped into my cranial spreadsheet: "Exceptional Circumstances" followed by "Grievous Ethical Alternative."

I then thought about exceptional situations with regard to international conflict. What do you do if another country launches a frontal attack on your own—dropping bombs on, well, Honolulu, an obvious spot to contemplate given Brian's journey to join us? What do you do when a regime is engaging in wholesale ethnic cleansing—eradicating a whole people from the face of the earth? Does Jesus' "turn-the-other-cheek" strategy apply here? Or does the command to choose life actually need to be adapted to the presenting circumstances to the point of even using weapons and death to accomplish a higher life-giving end?

Serving a church adjacent to the Patrick Air Force Base, whose members included many who served on the eastern missile test range, had already afforded me an extensive education in military deterrence as a strategy not for war but for peace. Oh, I personally favored disarmament, but I could not deny the sincerity of faith on exhibit whenever these deeply Christian church members would wax eloquent on the subject. Such discussions had prompted me to do some in-depth study of Augustine's just-war theory, which, on the one hand, affirmed the intentions of those advocating military deterrence yet, on the other hand, put defining limits on them. Surely, in times of international attack or ethnic cleansing, engaging in war could be a grievous ethical alternative to choose.

Then my mind wandered to the matter of crime and punishment. Yes, millions are doing time for crimes of all kinds, most, though not all, of them being guilty as jail birds, as the old saying goes. But what about those who have tortured and killed innocents? What about serial killers? What about the evildoers who have carried out such crimes and show no remorse?

A text from the book of Leviticus came to mind (not that I had it memorized, but the gist of it was clear to me):

> Anyone who kills a human being shall be put to death. Anyone who kills an animal shall make restitution for it, life for life. Anyone who maims another shall suffer the same injury in return: fracture for fracture, eye for eye, tooth for tooth;

the injury inflicted is the injury to be suffered. One who kills an animal shall make restitution for it; but one who kills a human being shall be put to death. You shall have one law for the alien and for the citizen: for I am the LORD your God. Moses spoke thus to the people of Israel; and they took the blasphemer outside the camp, and stoned him to death. The people of Israel did as the LORD had commanded Moses. (Lev. 24:17–23)

Now, I hate the death penalty. When asked to serve on the jury of a high-profile murder trial, I begged off, stating that I could not vote for a death sentence, no matter how evil the act and how totally confident I might be about the alleged perpetrator's guilt. I'm just too questioning of the possibility that the judgment might be wrong, that the evidence was not completely researched, or that the perpetrator stands too far out of redemption's reach to be saved.

Nevertheless, to be honest, while any lost life is tragic, I didn't weep when Osama Bin Laden was killed by U.S. soldiers or when Timothy McVeigh, the Oklahoma City bomber, was executed. The scale of justice is balanced by the eye-for-an-eye model. And, accordingly, in extraordinary circumstances the execution of such a perpetrator can be justifiably argued to be a grievous ethical alternative to life.

So what about problem pregnancies? A battle royal has been waged over the right of a woman to abort an unwanted fetus or, should I say, over the right of an unborn child to be carried to term and to be delivered into loving arms. Such positions have generated a passionately polarized debate.

Right to Life? Right to Choose?

The absolutist positions—the right of the child to live, even if the mother loses her life in the process, or the right of the woman to abort the fetus up to the time of birth—are supported by a relatively few people. Most Americans hold to a position somewhere in between those two options, even if absolutists argue for the absolute "right to choose" or absolute "right to life" in tones of absolute certitude.

Right to choose? Well, what if the choice is to avoid embarrass-ment, to avoid an inconvenience, to keep working at getting the gender of choice, and/or to make such a decision when the child has developed well into viability? Many pro-choice advocates will acknowledge that some women are making choices for unthinkably vain and selfish reasons and that the right to choose ought not to be exempt from the critique of second opinions.

Right to life? Well, what about a pregnancy that is threatening the life of the would-be mother? What about conceptions caused by rape or incest? What about the sure knowledge that the fetus is profoundly and severely damaged, guaranteeing zero quality of life for the child if carried to term? In at least some of these cases, many a pro-life advocate will leave room for an abortion to be an accept-able option. Such a caveat seldom gets voiced openly, since it flies in the face of the essential arguments that the person is a life from the moment of conception and, therefore, has a right to live. But com-mon sense does seem to beg for some leeway.

My mental spreadsheet quickly added these kinds of excep-tional situations, including the really hard-to-swallow "termina-tion of pregnancy" (a just slightly less harsh-sounding euphemism for abortion), to the "Grievous Ethical Alternative" column. As I drove up South Hickory Street and pulled into the parking lot, the final spaces in the spreadsheet now became obvious. The notion of measuring death not by a beating heart but by brainwave activity was a very new idea at the time. It was positing amendments to standards for medicine and for law enforcement. We were real-izing that brainwaves give a much better assessment of a person's vivacity and viability—especially in light of the increasing ability to revive stopped hearts.

A 90-percent-brain-dead assessment seemed to have an obvious implication for Ginger's future. Now with a life-and-death ethic chart drawn in my mind's eye and the dominion covenant empow-ering me to speak up, I realized just what I needed to say to Brian when we met in his mother's hospital room. Of course, I didn't think through all of these angles in all this detail in a fifteen-minute drive. Some of these insights developed over subsequent weeks and months and years.

Rule of Law, Rule of Love

One of those insights came when comparing this sequence of thought to the teleological-deontological dichotomy we discussed earlier in this book. On the one hand, each of these life-and-death decisions is law driven (deontological)—built on the organizing principle "Love your neighbor as yourself" and following the particular aspiration "Choose life." Specific standards or benchmarks apply:

- Turning the cheek and/or fleeing from the threat
- Negotiating for peace
- Prosecuting and incarcerating unto restitution, reconciliation, and rehabilitation
- Carrying to term (possibly to place up for adoption)
- Providing medical care and comfort

Then again, given extraordinary circumstances, we have turned our thoughts in the alternate direction, the "end-in-view" (teleological) direction. We have pressed ourselves to ask, "What is the loving thing to do when facing such extreme situations?" All of that has opened the door to the possibility of grievous ethical alternatives, what we've dubbed approximations and adaptations.

We have integrated the rule of law with the rule of love. In the process, both have been served—or, more exactly, both sets of principles have been upheld for our continued considerations for future life-and-death decisions.

Fearful Considerations

One insight emerged soon after this drive to the hospital. I determined then and there never to write about this subject until after retiring—in the mid-to-late 2020s. I knew that this spreadsheet alone would make me a pariah among my pro-life, antieuthanasia friends. I knew I'd be shunned by my anti-war, anti–capital punishment friends.

I have mostly stuck to that determination not to publish any of these ideas for over twenty-five years. To date I've written nearly three hundred editorials without ever going down this road. Yet the partisan extremism in both state and church and the rapidly shrinking respect being accorded the church for its blurting simplistic black-and-white answers to the younger generation's complex, full-spectrum-color-filled questions have pressed me to put the ideas inspired by Ginger out into the public conversation.

One other reason I kept these ideas to myself for so long was that I have found them to be difficult to abide. In fact, if you're breathing a sigh of relief over the presentation of this chart of ethical thinking, then you're missing the key part. You're missing the fact that every life–and-death decision is, indeed, a life-and-death decision. Every such situation requires us to face the horrors of its implications. None of these choices is a happy one; none can be entered into lightly—even those, such as self-defense, that require a split-second pivot and shoot.

Then again, eventually I did feel compelled to publish this experience and other thoughts that it launched. Gradually, over two-plus decades' time, this reasoning around matters of life and death morphed into the framework of overall biblical interpretation I'm now labeling integrative Christian ethics. With years of study I fearfully countenanced and then formulated and then began to proclaim an overall interpretive grid for reading a massive and holy book like the Bible. Eventually general terms grew out of my fifteen-minute drive to the hospital on that morning:

- "Be fruitful, multiply, replenish" grew into "aspirations."
- "Turn the other cheek; negotiate for peace; carry to term, etc." grew into "standards/benchmarks" and "applications."
- "Subdue" became "grievous ethical alternatives," which grew into "approximations and adaptations."

And, accordingly, I have felt compelled not only to tell Ginger's story but also to present this overall approach to discerning God's will in the most heart-wrenching circumstances.

A Conscience Informed by Community

Turn back to the previous chapter, and read again the central importance of being a part of, a student of, a promoter of, and a builder of a community of character, of disciple making, of the cultivation of informed consciences, and of shared decision making. Revisit the need to be engaged within your microcommunity, your congregational community, and your metacommunity while walking down these dangerous roads. Hold on to the others who can provide you loving support, wise counsel, and gracious forgiveness to deal with the aftermath guilt and pain that such choices leave behind.

End of the Story

All of which takes me back to that encounter with Ginger and Brian in the hospital that Monday morning. I strode a bit more confidently into the ICU, and there he was. Brian had arrived two hours earlier than planned, nearly a full hour before me. I shook his hand, looking at him, immediately conveying, as only the eyes can, the depth of my empathy for him and his mom.

"She's gone," he said. "I told the doctor to disconnect the respirator, and she breathed her last at that very moment." Oh, wow. I had dreaded the thought of her dying, but I was happy she was now free from pain. I felt cheated that I wasn't there, but I was glad that I didn't have to be or even share in the task of being "the decider."

For the moment all I could muster was "I'm sorry." And then to offer a hug. And then, "I'm so sorry." But then I quickly morphed into the part of pastoral care in which I was no novice: talking with him about his deceased loved one, sharing and inviting the recitation of memories—jotting down notes to keep in mind for the next few days of services, talking with him about the process of grief and about the ways I and my congregation wanted to walk with him through the emotional process of letting Mom go into God's arms.

The end of the story is that a few days hence I had the privilege of leading Brian, his out-of-town relatives, and many friends from near and far in a service of the resurrection. I proclaimed that the light and life of Christ have overcome the darkness and death that, apart from him, would have the final word.

I was able to remind my community of faith that the pro-life message we proclaim is one that rises above the life that is measured in minutes, months, and decades to one measured in the eternal present that is God. I also was entrusted with a spreadsheet, which I now share with you (see table 3).

Table 3: Pro-Life? Pro-Choice? Or Pro-Ethical?

Situation	Aspirational Benchmark Response	Extraordinary Circumstances	Grievous Ethical Alternative (Adaptation)
Self-defense / Defense of another	Turn the other cheek; flee	Life-threatening to you or the other	Self-defense: possibly even kill
International conflict	Negotiate, reconcile	Foreign invasion; evil empire	Just war
Crime and punishment	Incarceration, restitution, rehabilitation	Capital crime, repeat offender, no sign of remorse	Capital punishment
Problem pregnancy	Carry to term; maybe place up for adoption	Rape, incest, severe deformities, danger to mother's life	Abortion
Deteriorating health	Medical care, hospice care	Prolonged suffering; no hope of recovery; supported by artificial means	Discontinue life support

8

Love and Marriage

So here we are, wrestling with some of life's greatest questions. You and I are trying to do right, to follow God's will, to be ethical and moral and compassionate and faithful and courageous and wise. And in order to do and be all of those things, we are owning up to the fact that God's will isn't always obvious or even terribly consistent.

Then again, we are also asserting that God does deliver broad-sweeping directions for our living, beginning with the love commandments: Love the Lord your God with all of your heart, all of your soul, all of your mind, and all of your strength; and love your neighbor as yourself. We have delineated fourteen aspirational commands that give more specificity to the two love commandments (seven for each), and we've gotten more specific by summarizing the standards that serve as benchmarks against which we measure how close to the mark we are to each of those fourteen aspirations.

In turn, we have outlined ways that those benchmarking standards are most commonly applied in our faith communities—acknowledging some diversity of standards that reflect the diversity of our different communities. And we have shown how biblical figures and writers allowed room for approximations and adaptations and how such approximations and adaptations have continued to emerge in subsequent eras, including our own.

In chapter 7 we tackled the most ultimate issues—life and death—first by affirming the aspiration to choose life. We spelled out the places where that choice gets tested—self-defense, international conflict, crime and punishment, problem pregnancies, and deteriorating health. We lifted up the standards for choosing life: to turn the other cheek (or flee), to negotiate for peace, to exercise disciplinary justice toward restitution and rehabilitation, to carry the baby to term, and to provide quality medical care toward healing.

But we also named the extraordinary circumstances that called into question whether those standards must be followed exactly all of the time. In fact, we showed some approximations and adaptations taken within the Bible in three of those contexts—each of which allowed for death to result. Then we applied them in two other realms not explicitly approved in Scripture but where we found an equivalence that can become an ethical and faithful option, albeit a grievous one.

These insights have been shared with fear and trembling, knowing that they can be twisted into rationalizations that cannot be justified. Still, I make these claims because I believe that they reflect biblical teaching about life and death.

Where Angels Fear to Tread

Speaking of fear and trembling, I now rush in—no, change that: I now *crawl* in—where angels fear to tread: to the topic of human sexuality. No subject is prompting more argument within Western churches than that of sexual intimacy. Many a denomination, many a congregation, and many a Christian friendship have been torn apart by differences of opinion on matters related to marriage and the family.

Let us consider this human relationship matter under the aspiration "Be faithful." As a general aspiration, faithfulness is an essential attribute of God as is affirmed in the following Scripture passages:

- **The Law:** "Know therefore that the LORD your God is God, the faithful God who maintains covenant loyalty with those who love him and keep his commandments, to a thousand generations." (Deut. 7:9)

- **The Psalms:** "Your steadfast love, O LORD, extends to the heavens, your faithfulness to the clouds." (Ps. 36:5)
- **The Prophets:** "The steadfast love of the LORD never ceases; his mercies never come to an end; they are new every morning; great is your faithfulness. (Lam. 3:22–23)
- **The Apostles:** "God is faithful; by him you were called into the fellowship of his Son, Jesus Christ our Lord." (1 Cor. 1:9)

Aspirational Components of Faithfulness

But for those who were created in God's image, who at the beginning were made to partner together, what does faithfulness looks like? It's complicated, but its complications can make better sense and get sorted out by delineating the component elements, the sum of which comprises the overall aspiration to be faithful. This aspiration is comprised of seven components that are loosely sequential:

1. Purity of heart and mind
2. Chastity in singleness
3. Suitability in partnering
4. Mutuality in relating
5. Fidelity in monogamy
6. Generativity in parenting
7. Longevity through life

Let us survey the biblical mandates for these components one at a time.

1. Purity of heart and mind: In the opening section of his Sermon on the Mount, Jesus spells out the Beatitudes, the sixth of which says, "'Blessed are the pure in heart, for they will see God'" (Matt. 5:8). About twenty verses later, he specifically applies that ideal to sexual relationships: "'You have heard that it was said, "You shall not commit adultery." But I say to you that everyone who looks at a woman with lust has already committed adultery with her in his heart'" (Matt. 5:27–28). Of course, Jesus did not invent this notion. The Ten Commandments include the prohibition, "You shall not covet your neighbor's wife, or male or female slave" (Exod. 20:17b).

2. Chastity in singleness: In Paul's earliest writing, the First Letter to the Thessalonians, he says,

> For this is the will of God, your sanctification: that you abstain from fornication; that each one of you know how to control your own body in holiness and honor, not with lustful passion, like the Gentiles who do not know God; that no one wrong or exploit a brother or sister in this matter, because the Lord is an avenger in all these things, just as we have already told you beforehand and solemnly warned you. For God did not call us to impurity but in holiness. (1 Thess. 4:3–7)

3. Suitability in partnering: The basic plan for partnering is laid out in the biblical report of humanity's beginnings:

> Then the LORD God said, "It is not good that the man should be alone; I will make him a helper as his partner." . . . And the rib that the LORD God had taken from the man he made into a woman and brought her to the man. Then the man said,
>
> > "This at last is bone of my bones
> > and flesh of my flesh;
> > this one shall be called Woman,
> > for out of Man this one was taken."
>
> Therefore a man leaves his father and his mother and clings to his wife, and they become one flesh. And the man and his wife were both naked, and were not ashamed. (Gen 2:18, 22–25)

This language is echoed in Jesus' words in Matthew 19.

Suitability comes with some prohibitions, too, particularly in the matter of religious compatibility. Many times in the Hebrew Scriptures, the children of Israel are prohibited from intermarrying with people of other religious groupings. Paul echoes that selectivity for those in the early church:

> Do not be mismatched [commonly translated "unequally yoked"] with unbelievers. For what partnership is there between righteousness and lawlessness? Or what fellowship is there between light and darkness? What agreement does Christ have with Beliar? Or what does a believer share with an unbeliever? (2 Cor. 6:14–15)

4. Mutuality in relating: While the Bible often tells stories of dysfunctional marriages, it also lifts up the ideal of love and mutuality between partners. From the love between Abraham and Sarah to that of Mary and Joseph, a beauty of mutuality jumps out for all to note. Such mutuality is presented in clear relief in Paul's response to some Corinthians who were advocating for sexless marriage:

> Now concerning the matters about which you wrote: "It is well for a man not to touch a woman." But because of cases of sexual immorality, each man should have his own wife and each woman her own husband. The husband should give to his wife her conjugal rights, and likewise the wife to her husband. For the wife does not have authority over her own body, but the husband does; likewise the husband does not have authority over his own body, but the wife does. (1 Cor. 7:1–4)

5. Fidelity in monogamy: The most obvious teaching on marriage is that of "forsaking all others" (as expressed in many wedding vows in recent centuries) to share a monogamous relationship as spouses. Spelled out in the Fifth Commandment, "You shall not commit adultery" (Exod. 20:14), it is reiterated scores of times throughout the Bible.

6. Generativity in parenting: Those first words of God to the humans, discussed at length in the previous chapter, stress generating life: "Be fruitful and multiply, and fill the earth and subdue it" (Gen. 1:28). The psalmist echoes the joy of bearing children:

> Children are a heritage from the LORD,
>   offspring a reward from him.

> Like arrows in the hands of a warrior
>   are children born in one's youth.
> Blessed is the man whose quiver is full of them.
> They will not be put to shame
>   when they contend with their opponents in court.
>   (Ps. 127:3–5 TNIV)

7. Longevity through life: The clear assumption in Scripture is that the uniting of couples is intended as a lifelong, covenanted commitment:

> "For I hate divorce, says the LORD, the God of Israel, and covering one's garment with violence, says the LORD of hosts. So take heed to yourselves and do not be faithless." (Mal. 2:16)

Jesus echoes the plan for permanence several times, the following being typical:

> He answered, "Have you not read that the one who made them at the beginning 'made them male and female,' and said, 'For this reason a man shall leave his father and mother and be joined to his wife, and the two shall become one flesh'? So they are no longer two, but one flesh. Therefore what God has joined together, let no one separate." (Matt. 19:4–6)

Altogether, these Scriptures set forth the general plan for marriage that has been largely sustained in the Christian era. "But wait a minute, what about so-and-so or such-and-such?" you may say. And what you're likely to say probably is true. Exceptions abound in the Bible and in church life through the centuries. But that, in fact, comes back to our basic thesis that, on the one hand, the aspirations and standards/benchmarks call us to a higher life of holiness and godliness, while in Scripture and in life we run into situations that don't match. More on that upcoming. Let's now work through each of these components and see how they actually play out.

Purity of Heart and Mind

Yes, Moses forbade coveting a neighbor's spouse. Jesus prohibited lust altogether. So what has the church taught through the centuries? Basically, the same thing: Love is good; lust is bad. That has been the standard, the benchmark through the Christian era. And the church has generally applied that standard by promoting restraint for the unmarried in all matters sexual: dressing modestly and avoiding tempting influences both in public and in private. But then life happens. It's called puberty. And there's the sexually charged media and overall culture. And provocative dress styles. And muscle development. What's more, our understanding of psychosexual development has increased.

Here is a question for the parents of teens: Would you feel pleased if your eighteen-year-old reported that she or he has never felt any sexual desire? Perhaps in the Victorian Age folks would have rejoiced, but few parents today would blush with joy over that knowledge. They would worry that something was developmentally wrong with their child. In spite of what Jesus said, we expect lustful desires to arise in all adolescents.

What most of us do is either pretend that Jesus never said that, or we intuitively adapt it to the real world of our time and place. We have embraced the healthiness of sexual feelings and tried to channel that energy in other ways. In fact, effective youth ministries organize learning and social activities for teens to redirect the hormonal energy coursing through their students. The cultivation of multiple friendships and platonic relationships across the genders is both a strategy of adult mentors and a gift to the students themselves. And given that the marrying age keeps increasing (more about this ahead), raging hormones pose a massive challenge.

I recall when, as a teenager earnestly pursuing a life of Christian discipleship while also being in a romance waiting to happen (I did date regularly from middle school until my post-college wedding day), I heard simple advice from a youth director: the first look is human; the second look is sin.

Chastity in Singleness

"Believing that true love waits, I make a commitment to God, myself, my family, my friends, my future mate and my future children to be sexually abstinent from this day until the day I enter a biblical marriage relationship."

So goes the pledge taken by several million adolescents as a part of the "True Love Waits" movement. The organization by that name, formed in 1993 by Southern Baptists and soon thereafter supported by churches ranging from Roman Catholic to Assemblies of God, invites students to commit themselves to maintain their virginity until their wedding day. Many of those young people accept and wear a "promise ring," given by a parent to give witness to their good intentions.

No matter what one thinks about these efforts, they do reflect the classical conviction of the church. Sex should be enjoyed on the honeymoon, not before. But, then, life happens. The onset of puberty is arriving one to two years earlier than in decades past, although the reasons for that are not clearly known. Weddings get delayed until the mid to late twenties (the average age for first marriages in 2010 topped twenty-six for women, twenty-eight for men)[1]—largely due to greater emphasis on higher education and the availability of birth control and thus the ease of postponing childbearing. Accordingly, the determined efforts to maintain one's virginity need to persevere nearly two decades on average.

What does the apostle Paul say? "To the unmarried and the widows I say that it is well for them to remain unmarried as I am. But if they are not practicing self-control, they should marry. For it is better to marry than to be aflame with passion" (1 Cor. 7:8–9). Interesting that he did not simply command singles to "stop lusting." He certainly accepted the reality that sexual desire does long for intimate expression. In fact, whereas Paul is elevating the ideal of singleness, he is also the adaptationist: he supports the option to marry with the sexual intimacy that accompanies it.

---

1. "Median Age at First Marriage, 1890–2010," InfoPlease, http://www.info please.com/ipa/A0005061.html.

So what do most single Christians eventually do as they reach their late teens, their early twenties, or their mid-twenties? They try to maintain their chastity to a point, but then they adjust their expectations of themselves and/or the young adults in their circle of influence: they aim for monogamy and practice safe sex. And they try to resist feeling condemned with guilt. Those are the approximations and adaptations many make.

Then again, while older generations worry about the absence of young adults from church, the little-told story is that the absence of twenty-somethings has worried older generations for decades. We forget that their absence has been influenced by the large number of singles who are less tied down than those married, especially those married with children. What is not generally studied, and may never be since it would be hard for many to admit it, is the likelihood that many young, single adults are sexually active, and going to church just plain makes them feel guilty.

No simple solution presents itself, except for the church possibly to acknowledge the good intentions of those approximating and adapting the standards as best they know how. We all are approximaters and adapters.

Mutuality in Relating

The tender, affectionate, romantic, and sentimental side of marriage has long been intrinsic to the institution's existence. While many cultures couple together on that very basis, even those united by parental arrangement still look to marriage to become romantic and truly intimate (spiritually and emotionally, not just sexually) over time.

Some passages of Scripture lend themselves to setting out particular, different, but complementary roles for husbands and wives—drawn from the dichotomy of "Wives submit to your husbands. . . . Husbands love your wives" (see Eph. 5:22–32; 1 Pet. 3:1–5, 7). Some passages of Scripture lend themselves to truly equal status in the marriage, such as being made as "suitable partners" and joined together as "one flesh" (Gen. 2:18–25). Add to that the intensity of intimacy captured in the Song of Songs, and you get a picture of mutuality.

Whether in a "complementarity" model or "equality" model, mutuality is key. Both models require much of each partner, most especially sheer love for, care for, and honoring of the other. Abusive, overbearing, dominating spouses are sinning against God and the spouse—not to mention all others in the family and other circles of influence and impact.

Still, life does happen here, too. And in this case it generally arises in matters of difference: arguments, criticism, disenchantment, suspicion, laziness, taking advantage: all these issues and many more arise and challenge a marriage's mutuality. What to do?

Adapt. Many great marriage manuals focus on the need to "renegotiate" the terms of the agreement. The covenant of marriage into which a couple was joined included unstated assumptions and expectations, many of which were unrealistic then or became unbearable later on. By finding ways to renegotiate, couples in many a troubled marriage can find a new beginning. And the sour flavor in the throat can turn sweet.

Fidelity in Monogamy

So what is the traditional standard/benchmark for marriage if not an exclusive, covenanted partnering of a man and woman for life? Actually, as outlined above, the actual model is that of a virgin woman and a virgin man or, to be more specific, a virgin woman and a virgin man who have never had a lustful thought to consecrate an exclusive, monogamous covenant in a worship service and then to consummate that covenant together in a bed inside a tent or hotel room or home.

No marriages start out on such demanding standards. All are, at best, approximations and adaptations. Still, the expectation remains that the spouses will be faithful to one another for as long as they both shall live. That standard deserves to be upheld.

Couples need fortification from outside resources to accomplish and maintain such covenanted relationships. Accordingly, way back in the ancient world, worshiping communities became the officiants and consecrators of these covenants. Worship centers of virtually every religion perform weddings. The couples make solemn vows, exchange gifts and symbolic gestures—especially the almost universal practice of giving and receiving rings—and receive the prayers and well wishes of clergy, family, and friends.

In most countries, the state also adds its force of law to reinforce the covenant, to define the rights and responsibilities of each partner. An aggrieved party in the marriage can go to the courts to request enforcement of the covenant.

But then life happens. And so does infidelity. Now, we won't play counselor here. There are too many variables. From having a flirty conversation to having a secret life with a second family, marriages often get pushed to the breaking point. What to do then? Face the fact that the promise of perfect fidelity has been broken. You can't put that genie back into the bottle. Many marriages can be saved via apologies, forgiveness, prayer, counseling, recommitment, and building back the shattered trust. Some cannot or will not (in the latter case, see below under "Longevity through Life").

Generativity in Parenting

As outlined in the aspirations earlier in this chapter, the expectation that marriages will produce children is as old as humanity's origin and the creation mandate in Genesis 1:28. Having a quiver full of children (Ps. 127:3–5) has been a source of great joy, not to mention family proliferation.

Communities of faith as well as the forces of government have applied the benchmark of childbearing by fortifying the parenting processes through the promotion of nuclear and extended families. The family is the primary resource for children's growth and development. Accordingly, economic structures have been implemented to make home buying more possible, tax structures more advantageous, and medical insurance more affordable. And worshiping communities bless and consecrate all of life's major milestones—thereby adding force to the events and helping to create memories—what we used to call Kodak moments. But life happens. Infertility. Career orientation and birth control that make possible the option of couples not to bear children. Population explosion—even some countries' policies that limit the number of children allowed to be born.

For some, fertility clinics, a product of modern medical technologies, are a godsend, the means by which they can bear children. For others, adoption is the perfect answer. For still others, life entails any one or more of a billion other ways to contribute to the kingdom of God and to society in general.

Longevity through Life

As stated above in the "Fidelity in Monogamy" section, some marriages seem destined to fail. Then again, many persons trying to recover from a divorce are filled with guilt, shame, and a sense of failure. Hearing from Malachi that God hates divorce throws salt on the wound. What to do now?

First, let us acknowledge the aspiration to be united until death do we depart. And let's recognize the ways that faith communities and others apply their efforts to help couples accomplish that tall task: civil laws make divorce costly; ecclesiastical polity promotes reconciliation; and community approbation discourages marriage partners from rushing out the marital door. Obviously, many excesses of approbation have been produced (think: "bullying"), but still, some folks running headlong into divorce have been stopped in their tracks by loved ones' challenges, and some dying marriages have been turned around.

But life happens, and persons in bad marriages are faced with the awful possibility of going through a divorce. Like other topics already discussed, the church has often taken hard-line stances on the matter. The Roman Catholic Church still excommunicates divorcees unless they get their marriage annulled—a costly and difficult process. Then again, virtually every Protestant denomination treated their divorcees similarly until the 1960s. And conservative denominations did so well into the 1980s.

Divorced minister? An oxymoron until a few decades ago. Divorcees certainly were easily identifiable by the scarlet letter they wore on their cardigan sweaters. Ironically, such a stance was taken not out of a loyalty to Scripture but an unwillingness to read what the Bible really says about divorce. Conservative values overcame a passion to be biblical. The fact is, the two major voices in the New Testament to speak out for the permanence of marriage—Jesus and Paul—both understood that life happens. They offered approximations/adaptations to cope with the life that comes along.

In as central an event as the Sermon on the Mount, Jesus offered adaptions to the usual standard":

> "It was also said, 'Whoever divorces his wife, let him give
> her a certificate of divorce.' But I say to you that anyone who
> divorces his wife, except on the ground of unchastity, causes
> her to commit adultery; and whoever marries a divorced
> woman commits adultery." (Matt. 5:31–32)

On the one hand, Jesus strengthened the import of the existing prohibition against divorce. On the other hand, he opened the door to the
adaptation, allowing the faithful spouse to divorce the unfaithful one.

In a similar vein, Paul also affirms the standard of marital
perseverance:

> To the married I give this command—not I but the Lord—
> that the wife should not separate from her husband (but if
> she does separate, let her remain unmarried or else be rec-
> onciled to her husband), and that the husband should not
> divorce his wife. (1 Cor. 7:10–11)

Paul even underlines the need to stay married to an unbelieving
spouse:

> To the rest I say—I and not the Lord—that if any believer
> has a wife who is an unbeliever, and she consents to live with
> him, he should not divorce her. And if any woman has a hus-
> band who is an unbeliever, and he consents to live with her,
> she should not divorce him. For the unbelieving husband
> is made holy through his wife, and the unbelieving wife is
> made holy through her husband. Otherwise, your children
> would be unclean, but as it is, they are holy. . . . Wife, for
> all you know, you might save your husband. Husband, for
> all you know, you might save your wife. (1 Cor. 7:12–14, 16)

However, couched with that argument, Paul faces up to the part of
life that happens and does so in the category of abandonment:

> But if the unbelieving partner separates, let it be so; in such
> a case the brother or sister is not bound. It is to peace that
> God has called you. (1 Cor. 7:15)

That is to say, if a believer is abandoned by an unbelieving spouse, the believer is not obligated to that unbeliever any more. The believer is free to be divorced and to seek remarriage. Note Paul's final statement: "It is to peace that God has called you." God's intention for marriage is an uplifting shalom, not a stifling ball and chain.

Note that it is also survival to which God calls. For a woman to be abandoned by her husband in the ancient world was to turn her over either to be dependent on her family of origin or to become a prostitute. With only very rare exceptions, women were not able to find gainful employment.

So if these two adaptations are acceptable by Jesus and Paul, what about other even worse situations? What about a person married to a spouse batterer? Or a child abuser? Or one arrested for drug dealing or prostitute pimping? Must the one stay married? Common sense screams out that these other behaviors are worse than abandonment or infidelity. Granted, if one takes the two exception clauses as exhaustive, then these other behaviors do not qualify, but if one takes the two adaptation clauses as examples—the most common forms of spouse abuse in the first century—then other forms of abuse, including ones unheard of in the ancient world (like selling child pornography), would also qualify as adaptations to the standard.

Given that other marital issues can lead to divorce court, it truly becomes a matter of a judgment call as to the legitimacy of someone pursuing both divorce and remarriage. We also would be naive to assume that in each of these instances the one party is totally innocent and thereby free to remarry whereas the other is guilty and therefore not free to remarry. The assignment of guilt is seldom that cut-and-dried.

Then again, even in those cases where one divorcee does bear primary guilt for breaking up the marriage by inexcusable acts, that does not mean that his or her behavior is unforgivable. In the range of God's grace, no sins are excusable, but all sins are forgivable. By the gracious redemption made available by the Savior, all can be forgiven and set free of the guilt and can begin again. The ending of one marriage and the moving on to another does not match the standard of "for as long as we both shall live," but by God's grace wonderful things can happen, and the affirmation, "It is to peace that God has called you," can be reality in the lives of many.

Suitability in Partnering

So now that we have seen that every one of the previous six aspirations and its corresponding standards/benchmarks is being lived
out in the realm of approximations and adaptations—and many of
them were instituted in Jesus' day—we turn our attention to the
most controversial matter in this book: the determination of who
can marry whom. The original answer was simple. God created a
human, and then after having declared everything in the creation
good, God says something is not good: "'It is not good that the man
should be alone; I will make him a helper as his partner'" (Gen.
2:18). That in itself is a remarkable statement, for it was made prior
to any act of human sin.

So God creates and then brings all of the animals before the
human, who names each one, but still "for the man there was not
found a helper as his partner" (2:20b). So God creates the woman
from the rib of the man, and the man says, "'This at last is bone of my
bones and flesh of my flesh; this one shall be called Woman, for out
of Man this one was taken'" (Gen. 2:23).

Of all of the great gifts those two got to enjoy, one that may be the
greatest yet most overlooked was that the choice of whom to marry
was easy, a no-brainer. The closest competitor was an orangutan! But
finding a suitable partner has, ever since, been one of life's greatest mysteries. Some societies have formulated processes for parents
to arrange and negotiate among themselves to join their children
together. Other societies have entrusted the choice to the adolescents and young adults to follow their own romantic inclinations.

Billions of times a couple has gone to a place of worship to commit their lives together, and some of their dreams have come true.
Others have turned into unbearable nightmares. Yes, when it comes
to coupling, life happens. For some, no partner is found. For others, the Guess Who's Coming to Dinner? syndrome unfolds. This
1967 American comedy-drama movie by that title—starring Spencer
Tracy and Katharine Hepburn, playing roles of husband and wife;
Katharine Houghton, their onscreen daughter; and Sidney Poitier,
the African American boyfriend whose appearance at her parents'
home was a bit shocking—tackled the controversial topic of interracial marriage.

If the movie were remade today, maybe it would be African American parents and daughter and her white boyfriend. At any rate, the original movie retold the familiar Romeo and Juliet story—how the parents' child falls in love with "not our kind" of person. At the beginning of 1967, "not our kind" usually meant, "not our color." In fact, seventeen states prohibited interracial marriage (twenty-four others that had once outlawed it had lifted the ban). Finally, on June 12, 1967, the Supreme Court ruling *Loving v. Virginia* overturned those antimiscegenation laws.[2] Most scandalous for persons of faith is that the seventeen states overruled by the Supreme Court run from Texas to Florida to Maryland, and then back to Texas—what is commonly known as the Bible Belt. Christianity's heartland was the most segregated. So much for the legacy of Christian America.

Back to the subject of marriage, when one's child introduces a suitor that doesn't match the dream the parents had for their child for whatever reason, the parents generally go through an emotion-racked dance. After the child and date leave the house, like a pair of machine guns mom and dad blurt to each other everything that can and will go wrong for the young couple. They cry together. They pray together with a fervor their praying has never before evoked. They meet privately with their child and report their concerns and plead with the child to cut off the relationship. They wrestle and struggle, and then wrestle and struggle some more. The child may, in fact, take their concerns to heart and break off the relationship. But then again, the child may say, "I love him/her; we're getting married whether you like it or not."

This emotional dance gets prompted not just by interracial dating but also by interdenominational romance. Even with the massive successes in ecumenism, marrying between denominations—especially between Protestants and Roman Catholics—still causes compatibility concerns. The dance certainly gets prompted by interreligious dating and marrying—Christian with Muslim, Jew with agnostic, Mormon with Pentecostal, and so on. Paul's words about being "mismatched [commonly translated 'unequally yoked']" (2 Cor. 6:14) come to mind.

---

2. "Anti-miscegenation laws," *Wikipedia*, https://en.wikipedia.org/wiki/Anti -miscegenation_laws.

In my dating years, this prohibition against interreligious dating was nonnegotiable. I dated quite a few girls, but each one was a devout evangelical Christian. When studying in seminary, I and most fellow seminarians declared that we would never perform interfaith marriages. We would have to draw the line there. But then life happens. Not many of us falls in love according to our family's set of qualifications. Is there something about the person you love that may not meet your family members' hopes and expectations?

Life happens also if and when someone's child falls in love with a person of the same gender. I do not know why some folks have same-sex attraction. At the time of publication, no particular gene has been identified that establishes one's sexual orientation or, for that matter, any other behavioral pattern. The nature-vs.-nurture argument continues to carry on, with the scientific community leaning toward scientific, biochemical causation, but much research suggests that, in fact, human physiology and psychology are so complex and intertwined that we will never be able to identify a singular first and compelling cause.

I do know, however, that most persons of same-sex orientation are telling the truth about themselves when they say that their yearning to love and be loved, to experience intimacy with a significant other, and to share the everyday experiences of life with another person consistently leads to someone of the same gender. (By the way, when I say that *most* are telling the truth, that's just because I think it naive to say all people of any characteristic are telling the truth all of the time).

I also know that all human sexual patterns of behavior, at their very best, are still being lived out as a collection of approximations and adaptations: from the redefinition of purity to the revamping of hopes for longevity; from our bending of the rules of singles' chastity to the hosts of options available around procreativity. No weddings are getting consecrated between a "virgin girl who has never had a lustful thought and a virgin boy who has never had a lustful thought." Not one of us has or ever will measure up to the truly biblical model for marrying.

Heterosexuals, myself included, who have championed prohibitions against the approval of homosexual relationships have been championing these prohibitions against behaviors to which we are not attracted. That's a bit too convenient for me to continue to promote in good conscience. Instead, it seems to me that, given our celebration of marriage as such a wonderful gift of God to humanity—one of the great expressions of common grace given all the world—that we married heterosexuals should not feel the need to hoard it to ourselves.

I also know that after going through all the ritual struggles with the "Guess Who's Coming to Dinner" syndrome, healthy family members finally come to the conclusion "Whom you love we will love." So it was for my wife, Barbie, and me late in the process of doing the research for this book. Our thirty-something-year-old daughter, Kelly, dated and fell in love with an immigrant, whom I will call Samir. Raised most of his life in the nation's capital, he is very Americanized. In fact, he is a die-hard Washington Redskins fan, a season ticket holder—which spelled trouble for them as a couple. Kelly is a Dallas Cowboys fan. And they both are very assertive, outspoken, and competitive. Through two years of dating they "talked trash" about each other's team in season and out of season. Together they were lots of fun—they argued like Lucy and Desi on the *I Love Lucy* show (you may be a bit young to remember).

They had another problem. Kelly is a Christian. Samir is Hindu. As they progressed from fun dating to exclusive dating to serious dating to talking about marriage, Barbie and I grew into the "Guess Who's Coming to Dinner" syndrome ourselves. We talked incessantly about their relationship. We prayed with fervor to God to bring Samir to the knowledge of Jesus or to lead them to break up. We spent time with them, building a relationship with him; he has great character qualities. Plus, at the time I had become a Redskins fan, too, so I would join in their banter, siding with him against Kelly—all in good fun, of course.

As they were getting serious, they argued about how they would raise children—whether Hindi or Christian. They fought tooth and nail. Finally he offered her a compromise: "You can raise them Christian if I can raise them Redskins fans." She agreed. Ah, yes, we thought, at least she enthusiastically gave Jesus higher status than the Cowboys!

But we struggled with the prospect of her being "unequally yoked" with an unbeliever or, in this case, a somewhat agnostic adherent to a pantheon of gods—yet one whose Hindi shrine sat so prominently in his living room. And all the more, as the family pastor, who long has been pledged to perform Kelly's wedding, I knew I would be called on to consecrate their marriage. I would be in the place of crossing a ministerial discretion threshold right within my own family—something I'd once said I would not do for anybody.

As all of these conversations were rising to a peak, Samir called to invite me to a Redskins game—and to come early to have breakfast beforehand. I knew he would be asking for my blessing to propose to Kelly. I accepted. Barbie and I continued our wrestling together and with Kelly. We finally said to her, "Whom you love we will love."

Sure enough, Samir and I met; he asked me for my blessing; and we discussed life-planning matters, vocational matters, and faith matters. He even expressed a real interest to understand Christianity. And he did affirm that children would be raised as followers of Jesus. I gave him my blessing. Two weeks later, when he was planning to ask her formally to marry him, they had a big fight. They broke up. And she moved a thousand miles away. He later married a Hindu woman. Kelly hasn't found the replacement Mr. Right yet.

I can say in retrospect that our process was challenging, but the conclusion was correct. A healthy family does say, "Whom you love we will love." But I've also been haunted by that conclusion. What if the person wanting to marry my Christian daughter wasn't a Hindu man but a devout Christian woman? Which is a bigger departure from the benchmark regarding marriage: a spouse of a different religion or one of the same gender? If our healthy family could say in the one instance, "Whom you love we will love," could we have said the same in the other instance?

Deference and Discretion

To put it simply, the healthy family shows deference to the couple who are in love and wish to live in a covenanted, loving, monogamous relationship, to have and to hold, for as long as they both shall live. And given that the church is also a family, properly called the family of God, it stands to reason that somehow, some way, we need to be able to say the same to our members and our children.

Accordingly, as my denomination has moved away from a policy of blanket prohibition of same-sex marriages to one of discretion—being left to the respective ministers to perform and boards of elders to allow the sanctuary to be used—I find myself in the right denomination. Ministers long have been entrusted to make the judgment call as to whether a couple is ready to be married; it stands to reason that that discretion also should be entrusted to them for same-gender couples. Church boards have long determined what services could be conducted in their respective sanctuaries; it stands to reason that that power of discretion would continue.

Showing deference to couples and granting discretion to ministers—that's a formula that makes sense. And to you who may be seeking to discern whether you are in love with the one with whom your future can be the brightest and your love, the most tender, these typed words are accompanied with prayers that you will discern well. I wish it could be as obvious for you as it was for Adam and Eve. But it's been complicated for all of us ever since we moved outside the garden. That's just the way it is. Table 4, "On Love and Marriage," summarizes the ways that our overall aspiration to be faithful in our sexual relationships and have our children do the same is translated into standards/benchmarks, followed by the appropriate applications, approximations, and adaptations.

Table 4: On Love and Marriage

Aspirations	Standards/ Benchmarks	Applications	Then life happens.	Approximations and Adaptations
Purity of heart and mind	Love: Yes Lust: No	Live lust free. Promote prudence in public.	Puberty and a sexualized culture	Cultivate safe friendships; limit, corral your lust.
Chastity in singleness	"Save yourself for marriage."	Limit affections to "intermediate intimacies."	Postpone marrying; extended adolescence	Better to marry than burn; be monogamous; use birth control.

(continued)

Table 4: On Love and Marriage (*Continued*)

Aspirations	Standards/ Benchmarks	Applications	Then life happens.	Approximations and Adaptations
Suitability in partnering	Seek spouse who is compatible and complementary.	Arranged or romantic strategies → suitable partner	No partner found; interracial romance; interdenominational; interreligious; same-gender romance	Informed conscience; defer the marriage choice to couple(s); leave marrying to the officiant.
Mutuality in relating	Love one another in full partnership.	Work together to find complementary ways to serve each other.	Signs of incompatibility; arguments; conflict	Renegotiate "terms" of the covenant; adjust expectations.
Fidelity in monogamy	Exclusive, monogamous marriage of male and female virgins for life	Churches consecrate; civil laws circumscribe; and marital affections consummate the marriage.	Flirting / lust / infidelity / addictive behaviors / conflicts / loss of trust / incompatibility/ loss of marriage	Attempts to repair, repent, forgive; but divorce may be necessary.
Generativity of children	Be fruitful and multiply: a "quiver full" of children	The nuclear (and extended) family as the essential unit of society	Infertility; the choice to limit the number of children—in some cases to zero	Adoption to gain child(ren); birth control to avoid or limit child(ren).
Longevity through life	Till death do you depart	Civil laws, ecclesiastical polity, and community approbation deter marital failures.	Abandonment; infidelity; abuse. Criminal behavior; incompatibility; personal failures.	Freedom and grace to divorce, remarry, and be restored to leadership in church/ community.

9

Letter and Spirit

So, here you have it: a set of spreadsheets to take with you wherever you go in order to guide your every decision. Just like Jesus' original followers took with them when they traversed the known world to "make disciples of all nations, baptizing them in the name of the Father and of the Son and of the Holy Spirit, and teaching them to obey everything that [Jesus] commanded [them]" (Matt. 28:19b–20a). Well, maybe they didn't have spreadsheets.

Then again, those original Christians did not carry a pocket copy of the 613 commandments of the Hebrew Scriptures either. They didn't even tote a copy of the Ten Commandments. Neither did they distribute student handbooks to corral the behavior of their disciples as is done in modern Christian schools and colleges. But they did develop a sophisticated understanding of discerning God's will. Yes, they determined, perhaps under the influence of the great rabbinical scholars of their day, that discerning God's will is not an exact science. It does not lead always or even usually to just one right answer.

Instead, the apostles and other early Christian leaders understood that discernment requires wisdom in judgment rather than perfect aim to hit the bull's eye of the one right thing. Yes, their methods were intelligent and faithful—not an exacting science but an *approximating science*. They considered all of the available data, from diligent study of the Hebrew Scriptures to analysis of cross-cultural diversities (moving from Jerusalem to Judea, Samaria, and the uttermost parts of the earth).

They set priorities. First and foremost, they sought to love God with heart, soul, mind, and strength, and to love their neighbors as themselves. They aspired to express that love in God-honoring and neighbor-respecting ways. They lifted up standards to guide the implementation of the aspirations, most of which they inherited from their Jewish forbears. They applied them—put them into practice—in ways habituated enough that they functioned as "best practices" as we would speak of them today.

Then again, as they spread far and wide the good news of Jesus' love, they made many adjustments, many approximations, many adaptations of the standards by which they were applying God's will. They did not jettison the basic forms and structures of those standards. Rather they assessed their options in their particular places and times against those standards, using them as benchmarks against which to measure possible variations on the themes. Tables 5 and 6, which both duplicate and complete the first two tables presented in chapter 4, reflect my attempt to summarize their thinking in ways that hopefully match their vision and can shed some light on yours.

While living their faith in those complicated times, they fluctuated between leaning toward a more rigid interpretation and application of the laws (e.g., the book of James) and a more fluid reworking of the standards (e.g., Paul's writings). They drew lines in the sand on some standards while dismissing others (e.g., the Jerusalem Council in Acts 15). Their variety of approaches caused controversy, case in point being Paul's arguments with the Galatians for tipping too far into legalistic rigidity and his scolding of the Corinthians for engaging in Mardi Gras–style debauchery. And even after the ruling of the Jerusalem Council, they were still arguing about the circumcision of male Gentile converts beyond the lifetimes of the apostles themselves.

Still, in the midst of those struggles, their focus on love and the aspirations of the faith helped them make the main thing the main thing:

Table 5: Loving God with Heart, Soul, Mind, and Strength

Aspirations	Standards / Benchmarks	Applications	Approximations and Adaptations
Glorify God.	Worship the Lord with people of God.	Participate in weekly church worship, with Word and Sacraments.	Worship via TV or Internet.
Fear/revere God.	No false gods, graven images, nor vain naming of God.	Repent daily from alien alliances, masters, dependencies, addictions, and God diminishments.	Enlist foreign ideas, practices for God; don't let your purity cause others to stumble.
Adore God.	Pray without ceasing; commune with God constantly.	Exercise daily discipline of individual prayer and weekly practice of group prayer.	Don't be so spiritually minded that you are no earthly good.
Trust God.	Believe in Jesus; entrust your whole life into his hands; and do not doubt.	In gratitude, demonstrate your faith via devotion and service.	Invest; plan for a rainy day, for retirement, etc.
Take up your cross; follow Christ.	Confess; forgive; and obey.	Submit to church accountability and discipline.	Incorporate ambition, initiative, and industry.
Put on the mind of Christ.	Be transformed; renew your mind; study the Word.	Participate in daily personal and weekly group Bible study; learn from multiple sources.	Study broadly; be informed from multiple sources.
Keep the Lord's Day holy.	Keep the Lord's Day holy, setting it aside for worship and spiritual renewal.	Do not work on the Lord's Day; enjoy rest, relaxation, and the rekindling of relationships.	Use the alternate rhythm of rest/ renewal if working on Sundays (e.g., ministers).

Table 6: Loving Your Neighbor as Yourself

Aspirations	Standards / Benchmarks	Applications	Approximations and Adaptations
"Do unto others what you would have them do unto you."	Be generous; serve strangers and enemies, widows and orphans.	Engage in and support missional outreaches and charitable causes.	Resist deception and addiction enabling; set priorities for constructive giving.
Tell the truth.	Tell the truth, the whole truth, and nothing but the truth.	Report the facts; give witness to the Truth (Jesus), and speak the truth in love.	Tell white lies for kindness' sake; exercise respectful caution when giving a witness.
Do justice.	Do justice; break chains of injustice.	Exercise distributive and disciplinary justice; promote just structures.	Share with care; avoid toxic charity; temper punishments with mercy.
Be a steward.	Treat all assets as God's property.	Tithe time, talents, treasure; recycle; care for the creation.	Consume resources as needed for good; enjoy the 90 percent.
Choose life.	Generate and protect life.	Avoid all kinds of violence; make peace.	Allow some grievous ethical choices for death.
Be faithful.	Join heterosexual virgins in covenant of marriage.	Affirm singleness alternative.	Support divorce/remarriage; give deference to couples' choice; grant officiants the discretion to marry "suitable partners."
Cultivate community: people of God, body of Christ, temple of the Spirit.	Build community of spiritual, moral, and missional transformation.	Exercise discernment within faith community; be leader in "earthly" community.	Engage politicized complexities; be loyal opposition; be conscientious objector via informed conscience.

Therefore do not let anyone condemn you in matters of food and drink or of observing festivals, new moons, or sabbaths. These are only a shadow of what is to come, but the substance belongs to Christ. . . . Why do you submit to regulations, "Do not handle, Do not taste, Do not touch"? All these regulations refer to things that perish with use; they are simply human commands and teachings. These have indeed an appearance of wisdom in promoting self-imposed piety, humility, and severe treatment of the body, but they are of no value in checking self-indulgence. (Col. 2:16–17, 20b–23)

In fact, those followers' writings about Jesus express an appreciation for ambiguity that stands in stark contrast to so many Jesus followers today. So many simply stick their heads in the sand—insisting on treating some Bible verses as nonnegotiable absolutes while pretending to themselves and others that contrary verses simply do not exist.

Today's absolutist thinking is one of the scandals of the modern Christian subculture. The intransigent, self-assured, hard-line positions simply don't work in people's lives. Instead, such preachers promote a schizophrenic disconnect between the cut-and-dried, simplistic, reductionist platitudes that pound pulpits and promote political platforms and the messy reality in which real people live out complicated lives in their full-color world.

The enthusiastic responses I have received to lectures and workshops on this subject suggest that there's a hunger to become regrounded in a faith that is both biblical and practical, that reflects the teachings of the prophets and apostles, and that works in the here and now. The most common response I hear is "That's how I make my decisions. I just didn't have the words to express it." They have found help to better preach what they practice.

One of my major hopes is that adults can pass on to their children and grandchildren a faith that is rich enough, deep enough, and thoughtful enough for the children to say, "This works!"; "This brings me close to God!"; and "This is a Jesus worth getting to know!!"

New Covenant

The Scripture text that has been begging to be expounded through-out this book and is arguably the basis of it all comes from Paul's Second Letter to the Corinthians:

> Are we beginning to commend ourselves again? Surely we do not need, as some do, letters of recommendation to you or from you, do we? You yourselves are our letter, written on our hearts, to be known and read by all; and you show that you are a letter of Christ, prepared by us, written not with ink but with the Spirit of the living God, not on tablets of stone but on tablets of human hearts.
>
> Such is the confidence that we have through Christ toward God. Not that we are competent of ourselves to claim anything as coming from us; our competence is from God, who has made us competent to be ministers of a new covenant, not of letter but of spirit; for the letter kills, but the Spirit gives life. (2 Cor. 3:1–6)

Paul was a radical if ever there was one. He had a radical trust in Jesus, whose good news he proclaimed far and wide. He also had a radical confidence that Jesus was extending and applying his new covenant into the lives of countless people well beyond Paul's abil-ity to control. Apart from sending letters periodically to encourage, challenge, and correct them, he trusted Jesus by the Holy Spirit to guide them.

In particular he trusted the new-covenant promise to be sure and true: that the heart of stone is being taken out of the believers and replaced by a heart of flesh (as prophesied in Ezek. 36:26) and that the laws of God are being written on the hearts and inscribed in the minds of God's children. What's more, he did what few biblically minded pastors would ever countenance: he lifted up the spirit of the law as better than the letter of the law. That's such a dangerous thing to do in a culture racked with so much anxiety about one another's behavior (especially that of children and grandchildren). Rather than give hard-and-fast rules to be obeyed at every turn, he said that such rules kill and that it's the Spirit that gives life.

I have written this text and developed these spreadsheets with guidance and feedback from many friends, both religious academics and regular Jesus lovers, trying to keep in mind a similar confidence of the new covenant. Oh, I haven't strayed too far from the letter of the law—listening for Moses' voice all along the way. In fact, I have strained my ears to hear Jesus' elevation of the law (challenging not just sins of commission but ones of omission, sins not just of deed but of thought and word, too). I have wrestled with the varying ways that the inspired writers of the Gospels, Acts, and Epistles have interpreted the kerygma—teaching—of the Savior they knew face-to-face. I have tried to reflect their intentions for us who are separated by two millennia and thousands of miles.

At the same time, I have sought to elevate the spirit of the law, the motives in the heart of God as well as in the hearts of human writers, so that any movement away from the standards to approximations and adaptations would be the kind about which I could honestly imagine the original writer saying, "That's right on! Preach it!!" My greatest hope and prayer is that when I stand before heaven's gate, God will say of this short book, "Well done, thou good and faithful servant."

Caution and Commission

Please do not take this approach to biblical interpretation as license to turn it into meanings that are self-indulgent. That would be a travesty, a heartbreak for this pastor. Please seek to honor the word and spirit in which it has been written.

Now, as you live between the "good morning" and "good night"—those bookends of your days—wherein you find your heart yearning for a goodness that dwells in the farthest reaches of your most heroic dreams and trying to apprehend that for which you have been apprehended in Christ, perhaps you will want to hold onto the words of the psalmist:

> Trust in the LORD and do good;
>   so you will live in the land and enjoy security.
> Take delight in the LORD
>   and he will give you the desires of your hearts.

Commit your way to the LORD;
  trust in him and he will act.
He will make your vindication shine like the light,
  and the justice of your cause like the noonday.
                                    (Ps. 37:3–6)

CPSIA information can be obtained at www.ICGtesting.com
Printed in the USA
LVOW07s0111140416

483508LV00015B/77/P